Also by Lynne Cockrum-Murphy

Stronger at the Broken Places: Heuristic Inquiry - Growing Up in Chaos and the Journey from Suffering to Self–Actualization

Living Hope –Steps to Leaving Suffering Behind

Unfolding the Mystery of Self is an autobiographical exploration of the self. Lynne uses her own life journey to explore her changing view of self, healing, and God. The resonance of the book, not just Lynne's words, but her actual presence coming through, touched me deeply. As she affirms her life, the reader is invited to affirm theirs. The book, perhaps as an extension of the author, has an energy that nurtures and supports its reader in a mysterious way. A must read for anyone thinking their life is trivial, looking to expand their view of spirituality, or understand their healing talents. Packed with anecdotes that will lead the reader to insight, the book invites us to review our own lives and consider moving forward into easy and effortless spiritual change.

Dorena Rode, PhD

I was intrigued by Lynne's story of her path toward enlightenment, and was especially taken by her story of tragedy when she was young. I admire her for staying on the path and making so much progress.

Bill Worth

Doctor Cockrum-Murphy has provided a personal road map for a spiritual journey to enlightenment for anyone willing to embrace the message. She has provided a gift that is a must read for all.

Lynda Hemann, PhD., LISAC

Dr. Cockrum-Murphy presents a practical and applicable model to integrate intuition, giftedness, and spirituality in daily life. She unifies the subjects of metaphysical spiritual practice and psychology through personal narrative, and suggests coherent and pragmatic methods for others to achieve and organize similar capabilities. This is a meaningful read for anyone who questions the validity of applying of preternatural abilities in helping professions.

Kathy Mohr-Almeida, Ph.D.

This is a book filled with heart and soul. Lynne gives many workable examples of shedding the layers of suffering to allow your true essence to shine. A must read!

MJ Caldwell, R.N.

Lynne's book is a real page turner as the reader sees how Lynne has, and continues to, evolve spiritually without apology. Lynne comes from vulnerability as we are invited to listen to her, and to experience this journey she shares. It is then up to the one holding the book to look into themselves for their own answers, on their own spiritual journey. Thank you so much for being willing to open yourself that we may see.

Rev Sandra Hopper

Unfolding the Mystery of Self

We Are Never Alone

Lynne Cockrum-Murphy, Ed.D., L.I.S.A.C.

© Copyright 2016, Lynne Cockrum-Murphy, Ed.D., L.I.S.A.C.

All Rights Reserved

No part of this book may be reproduced, stored in a retrieval system, or transmitted by any means, electronic, mechanical, photocopying, recording, or otherwise, without written permission from the author.

Paperback ISBN: 978-1-62747-402-3
eBook ISBN: 978-1-62747-330-9

Prologue

Some of us walk a unique, decidedly spiritual path. By choice, some us create a spiritual life without religion and stand on our own. In my case, I have chosen a path to Christ consciousness or enlightenment.

In the loneliness, fear and uncertainty of my teen years I found solace in spiritual teachings, eventually discovering that we are not alone. Now I know we have teams of supporters, angels, guides, teachers, family members and the many aspects of God guiding us the whole time. If we tune in we can hear, see and recognize them. Not only are we not alone, we are a thread in a great tapestry that is richer, because we exist. I came to rely on and trust the beautiful unseen beings and live in concert with them as I move towards my goal of self-realization.

Over the decades, many times I looked to others for guidance and direction; spiritual teachers always responded. When I questioned and wondered where I was in the process, I read the writings of some of the greatest teachers and drew from their knowledge. A few even categorized the stages of spiritual growth in their books. It felt awkward though studying the greats while considering myself much more ordinary than they. How could I aspire to live a life like Jesus, Buddha, or more recent greats like Mahatma Gandhi, Mother Teresa or Yogananda? I see myself as a much more ordinary American, female, teacher, and average citizen. What does the path to enlightenment look like for people like me?

On the whole this book describes some of my spiritual process and experiences in order to provide an illustration of a path less traveled and how I discovered we are never alone. Since we are in a time of ascension, more roadmaps and guides will smooth and shed light on the way for others and encourage us to continue seeking, practicing and recognizing we are exactly in the perfect time and perfect place right now. Even as I continue to move forward, releasing the illusions of this world, I delight in the joy of the present.

Acknowledgements

I thank the many wonderful beings of love and light who have aided me as I wrote this book. My life is blessed and perfect because of the many teachers, masters, angels and ancestors that guide me and because of God, that which illuminates me and makes all possible.

I also thank my writing coach, Tom Bird, my editor, Bill Worth, my ever supportive husband, Doug Murphy and my dear supportive friends – with special recognition to my Greatness Circle.

Table of Contents

Part 1: Spirit Surrounds Us 1
Chapter 1: Never Alone 3
Chapter 2: Who Am I? 7

Part 2: Messages 11
Chapter 3: A Dream 13
Chapter 4: Three Visions 15
Chapter 5: God Allows All 19
Chapter 6: Love 23
Chapter 7: Expanding Perspective 25
Chapter 8: In Dream State 29

Part 3: Growing in Awareness 31
Chapter 9: Peace without Effort 33
Chapter 10: Expanding Understanding 37
Chapter 11: Gurus, Teachers and Masters 41
Chapter 12: Magical 45
Chapter 13: No Mistakes 49
Chapter 14: In This Lifetime 51
Chapter 15: So Many Lives 55
Chapter 16: Concurrently 57
Chapter 17: Teaching 61

Part 4: Healing 63
Chapter 18: Healing Tools 65
Chapter 19: Healing Self 71
Chapter 20: Healers 73

Chapter 21: Feeling Their Pain 75
Chapter 22: Healing with a Touch 77

Part 5: Consciousness 81
Chapter 23: Surviving and Thriving 83
Chapter 24: Holy Spirit 87
Chapter 25: Joy 89
Chapter 26: Emerging 93
Chapter 27: Emptiness 95
Chapter 28: We are Perfection 97
Chapter 29: Dream to Reality 101
Chapter 30: Seeing 105
Chapter 31: Life as a Playground 107
Chapter 32: Unfolding Wings 109
Chapter 33: Revisiting Where is God? 111
Chapter 34: Meditation and Mindfulness 117
Chapter 35: Babaji 121
Chapter 36: Jesus 125
Chapter 37: Broadening Awareness 129
Chapter 38: New Possibilities 135
Chapter 39: Eternal Luminous Being 137
Chapter 40: True Self 141

Part 1:
Spirit Surrounds Us

Chapter 1
Never Alone

Actually we never are alone. We have guides, teachers, angels, and loved ones with us all the time. Plus we are part of All That Is (God), which means we are also connected to everyone, to all of life, all the time. There is no aloneness. There is only unawareness.

At the same time, when I notice that a relative who has passed has come in spirit to talk to me, I used to spend some time wondering, is it real? Am I making it up? Why did he or she come? Often when I did notice the spirit of an uncle, aunt or my grandmother, I was in the kitchen, doing the dishes or at my desk working. Those must have been times when my mind was open and more accessible. Usually ancestors do bring a particular message or offer to help with something.

Their visits also showed me how death really is transition to another state of consciousness; more like they left town and are out traveling, but not going to pull up in a car in front of my house. And I cannot go to their house any more, nevertheless they still exist. Their visits and communications in spirit is more like talking with them on the phone.

I wish we were taught from childhood that just because others do not see what we (sensitive types) see, or hear does not make it unreal. My grandmother told me her husband called her name from the bedroom after he died. She walked into the room and looked because it sounded distinctly like his voice, loud and clear. Most people have seen something out of the corner of their eye and thought someone was there, then dismissed it thinking it not possible.

We are not taught how to tune in and listen.

In 1981, my mom visited me after she had been shot and killed in a robbery. Her murder was a devastating, culminating event after my first twenty-five years of life, trauma, tragedy and family dysfunction. I had returned to her home north of Reno, Nevada to make funeral arrangements.

Shortly after her death, I was alone in my parent's house when I realized she was there too, standing in the doorway of the bedroom near me. I felt certain it was her. I did not know why she had come. I tried to talk with her, but could not hear her although I sensed her presence. Now I suspect she wanted to show me she was on the other side of the veil so I would not think she no longer existed. It did confirm my belief in life after death so her visit not only was valuable, but it also made me feel less alone and reassured.

My sister, Brenda had a similar experience the day after Mom died. She tells it in her own words:

> After the Medical Examiner had come to my work to tell me about the shooting and that Mom had died, a co-worker offered to give me a ride to where my boyfriend worked. My co-worker needed to stop and get gas. While I was alone and waiting in his pickup, I had a feeling like someone was behind me and was wrapping their arms around me, hugging me. I knew it was Mom's spirit. She was letting me know she was alright and that she loved me. I didn't hear her voice; I just felt warmth inside of me. I knew that she was finally at peace (after her whole life of difficulty, torment, abuse and loss).

The peace and reassurance we felt after Mom's visitations may have been a turning point after all the turmoil of our early years. These experiences were the beginning of a life of knowledge that we are never actually alone.

Today, I can switch my awareness from thinking with my mind to an aware state in which I sense the angels, teachers and my guides' presence. The nice thing about those kinds of changes in one's spiritual growth is that once they occur, the growth is permanent. The gracious energy of these beings supports me. I suspect some degree of this connection and support from them continues, all day, every day even without my noticing it. Anyway as I write, I sense their presence as a gentle energy, no pushiness or demands. Sometimes I see their wings and their light. Other times I hear them introducing themselves. Tuning into their presence helps alleviate the feeling of aloneness so many of us have. Today, I know in my heart of hearts I am never alone. We all have teachers and guides and angels and ancestors with us throughout our lifetimes.

The first time I remember being visited by nonphysical beings I was only two and half years old. Two blue angels visited me while I was in the hospital after surviving the house fire from which my dad rescued me, but died trying to save my two sisters. Once I had healed enough to be placed in a regular crib, I remember being alone and wondering what had happened. At some point, two blue angels stood at the foot of my crib and talked with me. They comforted me and eased my loneliness. Because these beings appeared no taller than the crib and my sisters had recently died, I decided they might be my sisters, Susie and Peggy. I wonder were they really blue or was that the calming, pain-relieving energy they projected towards me? Either way, their presence, and the possibility that they were my sisters and/or angels remains a demonstration of deep love and consolation and means a lot to me.

How do we become aware of the presence of these loving beings (guides, teachers and angels) all day? Part of it requires distinguishing their voices from our own thoughts. We hear their guidance from the day we are born; it takes conscious awareness and discernment to distinguish their influence from our own thoughts.

Development of discernment took me time and practice. Increasing the ability to discern took prayer too. I told Creator that I wanted the gift of discernment. I asked spiritual teachers what it was and how to get it. I read about it. Today, I still pay attention to what I hear in my head and determine where it came from – my own thinking, someone else's or something else. From there I decide if I will follow it, ignore it or do something else. Practicing awareness of guides and teachers by listening and asking questions, asking for signs, by paying attention and learning to discern their thoughts and suggestions from our own enriches our lives.

Shifting from wondering about these spiritual beings all around us to becoming certain of your experiences with them improves as you acknowledge all those moments when you thought you heard, saw or felt something that others did not notice or that you cannot see when you look directly. Acknowledge how sensitive you are and that your knowing and awareness is real, and that the beings you suspect are there are real too.

Chapter 2
Who Am I?

Who was I?

I remember fear, drama, self-judgment, anger, pain, while still being willing, open, and seeking, not sure what was possible, hoping and striving for inner peace. Part of me always believed the peace, joy and love I sought truly remained obtainable.

Recently, I struggled temporarily as fear came up because in the writing and publication of my previous book, *Living Hope –Steps to Leaving Suffering Behind,* I exposed the sexual abuse I experienced at the hands of more than one family member. I revealed getting married at age seventeen and divorced at nineteen. I acknowledged my drug use from around age fifteen to twenty-five. There was not much normalcy and stability in the first twenty-five years of my life, except for my paternal grandmother; she was a rock, stable, and nurturing. She provided unconditional love.

My mom went to work every day, appearing stable yet my life was interspersed with moving every school year, fathers and stepfathers dying, and family dysfunction. I went on to numb the pain as best I could by partying and by hoping to get the love I craved. Who wants everyone to know all that stuff? Men don't mind being known for promiscuity so much. They appear to be proud of it; in a woman it is still pretty much judged.

I put aside my fear of the readers knowing my family secrets through that book and moved forward; following the old saying "feel the fear and do it anyway". There has always been a part of me that compels me to do the work, the healing of self, the seeking of inner freedom. Courage, inner strength, faith and trust carry me when I am afraid.

The losses I experienced began at age two and a half, first as the result of our house burning down causing the death of my dad and two sisters. After that, I struggled for life with my severe third degree burns; this was followed by abuse and at age nine the death of my stepfather (in a suspicious logging accident). Advancing alcoholism in my mother and next stepfather all went together to create in me a deep loneliness and unhappiness.

Lastly, the cycle of trauma ended when I reached twenty-five years of age when my mom and stepdad bought a neighborhood bar and just two months later were robbed, my mom shot and killed and my stepdad injured. As a result of all of the traumatic events, all the suffering and loss early in my life, I felt at life's mercy, never knowing when the next person would die, never knowing when my life and those I love would be in danger again.

You can easily see how I ended up with a weak sense of self, a need to please others and a fear I was not enough. Plus I was unsure my mother had loved me and I felt terribly alone.

Who am I?

Still I experience a little of those old traits, but now I am also wise, usually at peace, certain the transformation of self-realization is gradually transpiring. There is such possibility in each of us. I love who I am becoming. My troubles lie in the past. The path comes easier most days because so much of my karmic slate has been wiped clean. Assuredly, I healed much of the past through traditional and nontraditional spiritual means. I know to use my healing tools regularly, particularly when I notice uncertainty.

Still on occasion I step into drama (usually with family), then step out, look back and laugh at myself. Earlier this year I got caught up in the drama of caring for an elderly family member. She made a huge, dicey financial decision that panicked me because I wanted her to do something much safer and reduce the risk she created.

She refused to hear me. She wanted what she wanted. I thought I knew what was better for her. Once I realized my buttons were pushed and I was caught in the drama and dysfunction (thanks to my husband speaking up) I quickly used the tools I teach others to use. I stepped into another room. I drew my attention inside myself and slowed my breath. I reminded myself that a drama was being played out here and yet this was not my reality, I stepped back (figuratively). Then I decided to step out of the role I had played. I still had opinions about the wisdom of her actions, but now I could live with them because they remain her choices, her life, and her consequences. With detachment, I can care.

Just a day later, I could laugh about it. I laughed at losing my awareness and needing to convince her to do what I thought best. Getting caught up in others' lives rarely happens to me anymore. Thank goodness I can get out of it quickly and regain my clarity.

Today I know I am loved, that my mother truly loved me and that I am lovable. It was a gradual process but it shows how doable that transition is - with persistence.

Today I create (books, art and song), I teach healing and spiritual classes, and I live knowing I am not alone.

Who will I be?

Even more empty, totally at peace, unattached to the illusions of this plane and unlikely to enter the drama. That is not quite it.

I suspect as I continue my spiritual practice my old pains and preferences will continue to fall away while the sense of "knowing" within each moment and each activity grows and governs my life. I imagine what I am coming to is realization of full consciousness which includes remaining in the state of stillness within daily life and activities. These inner changes will be reflected outwardly, physically too.

My, it is hard to say since I am not there. I expect more clarity, wisdom and light. I expect higher vibrations and the infinite being that I am to shine its transformative radiance into the world.

Throughout this book I share my process and show:
1. I believed in a force greater than myself (starting with the God I learned about in church as a child).
2. I believed it could change my life if I sought it.
3. I began seeking in my teen years.
4. I found what I desired and became whole.
5. In that wholeness I have much to offer others.
6. In that wholeness I reach and assist others through my spiritual strength.
7. The divinity of light and love flows from me and touches the world.

Part 2:
Messages

Chapter 3
A Dream

A spiritual practice produces many unexpected changes and after-effects. Little did I know when I embarked upon a spiritual path that I would talk to angels, channel messages, see visions, develop and accept all the wonderful and weird abilities that I now embrace.

I want to share a dream I had, much like a vision or even like a memory of something that had really happened in another time and place. The dream felt real and has created in me a fantastic desire to live some version of it.

In this dream, I was asked to join a choral group and sing at a performance where for some reason they needed another singer. Why they chose me I have no idea. I thought I would be part of a chorus, just blending in. So although not a trained singer and not prepared in any way, I agreed and went.

The whole event felt ethereal and took place in a huge, old, ornate theater. I discovered singing came naturally. I realized I had sung publically in front of large audiences before however the memories were vague. This experience also seemed entirely different from the past life I remember in which I was a male singer who traveled the mountains of Europe for my work. I do not think there was a connection between that life and this dream.

In the dream, I sang with an angelic chorus on the stage, and then apparently it was my turn to sing a solo. Yikes, I thought, really? Me? At the same time, the energy was so beautiful and everything felt so perfect, I began. As I sang, I floated off the stage and continued floating, moving up the walls almost to the ceiling, I thought how peculiar and yet it felt right. I had not studied the words. I did not have a part in particular that I noticed. I knew and sang God's words. My voice was very capable of all that was required although I remember thinking I was off key a few times yet the audience didn't flinch. The vibration of God expressed in song is what everyone recognized. I was awed by the experience. Sure I questioned the oddity of it all. Most importantly though, the audience loved the song. It felt angelic, yet I was me. The enthusiastic applause went on and on.

As I woke from the dream still feeling that amazing angelic energy, I was left wondering who I am. What was that about? Why did it appear I was an angel?

Contemplating the dream and my resulting desire to sing as God's voice, I realize the vibrations that come along with the song and the Holy Spirit touch and transform those listening. Those especially high vibrations heal hearts and minds. Song is one more way Creator touches, uplifts and changes us.

Chapter 4
Three Visions

Visions, a gift totally beyond my control, show up or they don't. Some visions appear in a flash, some take over my vision and remain longer than comfortable. Some show the future, or as with the last one in this section deliver a significant message.

The first vision occurred as I sat in the University of Oregon library in Eugene, Oregon and looked out the window. The not too distant mountains came to my attention. The mountains struck me as not being what I was actually looking at, but existing someplace else. I saw a distant place with brown dry mountains. At the time, the mountains surrounding Eugene were green and lush with forest and growth. Knowing I was seeing a vision different than my ordinary reality, I wondered, am I moving back to Nevada with all it's brown hills? I had lived in Reno from fifth grade through college. I did not have any answers and let it go. A few years later, after moving to Phoenix, Arizona, I noticed the mountains in the east valley and felt a click inside. I knew, "Ah ha, there are those brown, barren mountains." Back in 1984, I saw the future of where I moved in 1989.

A vision that totally obstructed my regular vision occurred while I was picnicking with members of a workshop my friend Nancy Ottis and I led in the area west of Vallejo, California in 1988. We sat on top of a hill looking out over a valley south of us. My vision switched from seeing what lay in front of us - the houses below us and a freeway - to seeing the whole valley filled with water. The valley became a waterway stretching out from below where I sat, filling the valley to the east, west and south. I did not get any messages from what I saw. I also could not look in that direction without seeing it. Ultimately, after using additional resources I realized I had seen the future of that stretch of land. The entire valley will eventually fill with water.

Another vision occurred during a visit to a Napa Valley, California spa. After a mud bath and a shower, I entered a small room for a massage. In front of my eyes, I saw Jesus kneeling at the rock at Gethsemane. In that moment, I knew his internal experience. He was aware of the pending sacrifice he faced while he also emanated his complete willingness to go forward with it. His knowledge of the purpose of the sacrifice, the meaning and the value of it made it all worthwhile for him. At that same moment, I felt that same willingness to sacrifice in order to serve humanity. He portrayed total surrender. This vision was important because years later I saw how the information about sacrifice and several past lives of mine that I remembered came together revealing a theme in my life.

During a visitation by my deceased father during an advanced healing class I attended, a practitioner showed me my family carried a gene of sacrifice in our genetic code. The programing for sacrifice came to my awareness and was cleared through the ThetaHealing® technique. (ThetaHealing created by Vianna Stibal, more information available at www.DesertJewel.org).

My understanding of sacrifice actually came from the Christ at Gethsemane vision and a series of two more that followed. In the one with Jesus, I sensed his willingness to sacrifice himself for all of mankind, a joy in serving God and trusting it would work. It didn't feel like sacrifice. It felt like an honor. A similar message came when I remembered my life as a beautiful bronzed-skinned girl with long black hair selected as the one to sacrifice herself in the volcano in order to bring good fortune for the village. It had always been done that way in that place and time. I/She felt honored to be the one even though it required suffering and death.

And finally I saw it in my own Dad, who sacrificed himself saving my life and attempting to save my sisters' lives. When I was two and half years old, our furnace broke, exploded and burned down the house. My sisters, Susie and Peggy died in the house. Our dad was unable to reach them. He sacrificed himself gladly for the love of his children. He died saving just one – me.

Not only did the visions give me clarity on my father's choice but also on my propensity to sacrifice myself when it truly is not necessary. I can give, I can serve, and I can act out of love. It does not have to cost me my life.

In fact, Christians teach that when Jesus lived and died sacrificing for all humanity, it was the end of a need for sacrifice. All the sacrifice of animals in the Old Testament was no longer necessary to please God. The greatest sacrifice of all came from God and that changed everything.

For me, the matter came down to clearing out old genetic programming keeping me thinking it necessary to sacrifice myself while I serve God. I am done with it now.

Although visions and dreams bring messages, some easily understood and others a mystery for years, they augment my life without direction from me. They simply occur.

Chapter 5
God Allows All

As I write it looks as if I am alone. I sense love, beauty and power and know I am supported by unseen beings of light. Midst all the amazing awe inspiring parts of life I find myself wondering about suffering. Why do we suffer? Why is suffering a requirement on this planet? Is it about creating? About experiencing? Is suffering meant to motivate us to get back to source, to our true selves? Misery certainly motivates me to take action and in particular to connect with Source and to open my mind to greater understanding.

In the same way, I use to question why a dark side and not only the light? Why do we experience duality here? We live with good and evil, life and death, right and wrong, all examples of duality.

I was taught as a child that Satan, an angel, fell from heaven and became a dark force opposing God. The church also taught that God sent armies to smite down evil. I always wondered if God is almighty why he had to fight. This is God we are talking about. God created everything and is omnipotent. Why would he have to battle? Now I can see I lacked a deeper understanding. That drama may not have been what actually was occurring.

As a child, I believed all the drama involved in Christian teachings. That and the general explanations of God as something powerful and beyond human understanding led me to think of God as something outside of me.

In the 1990s, I realized God allowed the whole occurrence when the angel Lucifer fell, became Satan and created a hell. God allowed it all. And now, my truth has evolved to believing that God allows us complete freedom of choice. The drama, the battles, they are our own creations. We create complex lives and relationships, cities and states and lengthy complex dramas intertwined with it all. That is us. That is free will.

We do not have to stay at this level of understanding. Beneath all the polarization, we are all God consciousness. Focusing on the consciousness that we are within and underneath all the thinking; that consciousness contains peace.

In considering the dark and the light, the duality, I wondered why we are here. Why are we so lost?

Recently I came across what a few others said about why we are here. Every religion has its own take on our purpose.

My personal mission statement has been to live a meaningful, purposeful life reaching others though my spiritual strength. That does not mean that is what my higher self would say. I came up with this mission statement about five years ago. It provides part of the picture explaining why I am here: it focuses on my intention of what to do with my time here.

Here is Shakti Gawain's take on why we are here:

We are here to learn to manifest spirit into physical form.

The spirit – or universal intelligence or experience of oneness – has manifested itself on earth in order to experience twoness. The universe wants to make love to itself. It wanted to have a relationship with itself. So it created a realm where we can experience, separation, individuality and difference and at the same time that sense of oneness that is always there underneath it all. We're here to learn about oneness and duality, merging and separating. We are here to learn to embrace both these principles, to be able to experience ourselves as one with the universe and at the same time as being unique manifestations of that universal source.

And here are Shirley MacLaine's thoughts:

"What if suffering is the way we choose to learn compassion? If we don't experience something ourselves, how can we understand what someone else is going through?"

According to Nancy Seifer and Martin Vieweg in *Living as a Soul:*

To live as a soul is to realize that everything of a material nature is transitory, including our physical bodies; that all things pass away but the spiritual Self never dies. To live as a soul is to be aware that we have incarnated before and will do so again and again, on the journey toward spiritual perfection. ... The particular reason may await discovery as one's life journey further unfolds. But learning to live as souls, collectively, is the evolutionary goal for humanity as a whole in the coming era—according to the modern wisdom teachings.

The Buddhist teachings say we have been caught in the cycle of life, death, and rebirth; living, suffering and repeating it all for eons. What a mess we have gotten ourselves into. Buddhism also teaches us how to step out of the cycle of karma and rebirth.

My spiritual teacher from the 1980s taught that after we as conscious beings separated from the totality of God Consciousness, we became separate beings. We behaved more like Gods at first, but later as we lived in the density of form, we gradually forgot who we are, forgot our connection to consciousness. This is another version of "the fall".

Actually, we never fully disconnect from Source because that which is our soul and in our cells is alive, vibrant and conscious, sometimes called God. Nonetheless, we grew dim, stupid and denser. As we work our way from the result (how we have been for thousands of years) we move forward and fall back too; all a long arduous climb out of ignorance.

Aren't we glad the awakening process has energetically increased now? The more support the better. I am tired of confusion, fear and karma. I choose, light, awareness and peace.

Definitive answers are hard to come by. We do receive nudges towards knowing. When we are not in a physical life on Earth, I suspect our knowing moves to an entirely different expanded level. For now we do the best we can to remember who we really are; we support each other and receive the guidance of many loving, unseen beings.

Chapter 6
Love

When I am channeling, healing, counseling and writing I know I am love. I sense a heightened degree of love, patience, understanding and acceptance. The entities that come to assist me at those times also are love. We are the same thing. I sense they love me. They cannot not love me because it is the essence of who they are. It is warm and soft. Love is not fierce; that is passion, which is different from what I feel. This love is soft like kittens, soft like wispy clouds after a storm, soft like the pale pink sunset, soft like a bird floating, slowly soaring over the ocean and soft like a dog's big eyes.

When I think of love, I think of how I learned about it while caring for my sister Brenda when she was a baby. I did not know I could feel so deeply about a person. It amazed me the first time I felt it; as if I did not know how beautiful love felt before. My intense feelings for her showed me the power and the sweetness of love.

Quite profound in my development of love and loving was the validation of my value through my grandmother. She wrapped me in love and was protective and consistent. I always wanted to see her and be with her. I could count on her. Thinking or talking about her today, and about how much I appreciate her role in my life, I still miss her and feel the loss. Funny though; she still visits me so I know she is not gone, she is simply different.

My dear friend of twenty-five years is love to me. This woman, MJ, although human, shows me unconditional love decade after decade. Our mother/daughter-like relationship is a challenging friendship at times but pure love always. Probably our genuineness and honesty with each other along with the support of each other indicates how important our relationship is to us.

Then there is my husband: as another example of unconditional love, a remarkable and constant thing. With him there have been rough moments too; gosh, we have over thirty years of marriage. On the other hand, I am so loved. He is amazingly supportive. His love and encouragement empowered me to grow, to challenge myself, face my demons and become who I am today. I go to him repeatedly for his wisdom.

What else is love? Kindness. Generosity. Love may not be defined as support, but it is often how love looks. My ability to love is consistent, but not perfect. It does not have to be. I am perfect within. I do not have to do life perfectly.

Chapter 7
Expanding Perspective

This message channeled from a larger fully conscious version of me draws a picture providing us an opportunity to expand our perception. The fourteen entities who came and shared the perspective in this experience prefer not to be known as separate entities. They speak as a group not needing to be named. They come from the same consciousness that I am (that you are). Here is a more developed version of what originally came forth for a client.

We are asked to imagine ourselves as a child, boy or girl, maybe four, five or six years old, sitting cross-legged on the carpeted floor in the living room of a comfortable home. You have a huge stack of Legos next to you and many more in a crate for you to dig into. Imagine how much you love creating with your Legos and letting your imagination run wild.

As this little person, first you build a house, and then you build more houses creating a village. You focus all your attention onto your creation. You imagine your family, you add more, all the people, animals, livestock, pets and trees. You give the people names and create stories about them and their families. You have their conversations. You are creating. For this moment, you are totally absorbed in this make believe world you created. You lose all track of time and go in deep, getting lost in the stories, the details and the drama. You love creating these stories, playing with the people as if they are real. Day after day, you play with your Legos and laugh out loud at your creations or get mad and tear the village down or cry when you have to clean them up and put the Legos away.

Mostly, you want to be lost in the story so you can pretend you are the knight, or the boy with the dog in a field, the princess, the fireman. You can save the world one day and destroy it the next. You are all powerful; a short god.

Now step back in your mind's eye from the scene on the carpet. Allow your perspective to expand. Realize you are also the parent of that child standing nearby, leaning against the doorjamb with a cup of coffee in hand watching the child play. You are pleased because you created, birthed and are raising this little person. You recognize his joy in creating and living through his creations, truly like you.

You laugh when he laughs. You feel his frustration when his crafting and constructing ends in disaster. You offer new tools or ideas when he fumbles in his play. You applaud his achievements. You delight when he accomplishes something new he did not know how to do before. Awe at his growth and development rises and catches in your throat.

You created this little one who creates. You manifested from yourself a perfect being, a god-like being that builds worlds and destroys them. You overlook the dramatic stories he invents, no judgment here. You see his innate self shining through, giving you joy as you watch him put his thought and desires into form. You know you are he and he is you. You are made from the same DNA and the same life force. His independence from you means discovery, inventiveness and potential. He is empowered to be all that he chooses to be.

You add to your own completeness as you witness your offspring. You are more than you were before this moment. You are grateful that you could birth this amazing, creative being and enjoy the evolution and growth occurring right before your eyes. Your life is deeper and richer because you witness your creation creating.

Now, expand your awareness and step back further still and see this scene from a limitless perspective.

This time notice you are not contained by your body. If you expand your awareness outside your body and keep going, look for the edges of yourself. Where do you end? Do you end or do you extend beyond this planet and into the universe? Do you sense that you are an infinite being? Are you huge, expansive, without end?

Possibly another perspective: you are also the space in the room, the energy in all objects and people. Sense yourself as existing in and beyond your body. You include everything. You are the awareness and the space between the objects, the child and the parent. You are not physical. You are consciousness, a life force aware that you include everything, aware of self as child, self as parent and even as the room and the objects in it. You include all that and have awareness of self at the same time.

What if you are now full cosmic consciousness? You, limitless and aware of self as the energetic life force in the air that surrounds these two people, one young, one older. Be the air that enters their lungs, the oxygen that moves into the blood stream and pulses through their bodies. What if you are this? Again, you are not physical. You live inside the physical and outside it. You include the physical, the people, the toys, the creations, the walls and the coffee cup. You are the energy inside the molecules, inside everything.

What if you were that life force? What if you are that which keeps the pieces held together in the chosen form? What if you are that energy?

You are actually all these things:

- Child who plays in worlds of his or her creation.
- Parent who birthed all that.
- The consciousness aware of all.
- The energy that brings it all to life and sustains it.

You are all that. Visualize, contemplate, and meditate on this as often as you can until it is obviously you, until it makes sense, until you know the truth of you. Allow that transition to evolve.

This message came one week before this book was started, channeled for the reader who is ready to hear it and the writer who lives more and more from this awareness.

Chapter 8
In Dream State

As we grow in awareness, we are more cognizant while in the dream state and remember more upon waking. Often traveling in our dreams is what we remember most. As a child in my dreams I would run until I'd lift up of the ground and be flying. In my 40's I always took the train and would return by train right at the end of the dream. In our sleep we visit planets, dimensions and receive visitors. The dream state is full of action, full of life; we just have difficulty remembering it and understanding it when we wake up. Is it changing for you?

New awareness has been showing up for me in the dream state. Often now I hear a short concise message and remember it. Most recently the message "Be Present" came through loud and clear regarding my habit of getting lost in thought. In other dreams, people show up asking for help. Deceased individuals come to me looking for the light and others come to me because of situations like the next example. All show how active and purposeful the dream state is.

Last night, I had a dream which alerted me to a problem I could resolve for my husband. While I was sound asleep he appeared in my dream and told me that earlier that day when he was checking on a client at the state hospital a bunch of negative entities moved from the car they were near, came to him and stayed with him. He asked me to get rid of them for him. Then as I woke up I could feel their icky energy that usually generates fear. I discovered six entities.

I originally was taught to think of them as negative entities, then by another teacher the term "fallen" and a different teacher more recently calls them "demons". I was able to send some of them on quickly and easily and had to sit up and call the Holy Spirit and really be awake and alert to send away the last particularly stubborn one. I made a point of not listening to their blathering, not allowing myself to get scared and always stayed strongly connected with Source and the light. Then the dark ones have no option but to go to the light. I prefer to offer the light rather than simply sending them away. I think it is wonderful that they can be transformed by the light into something more pure. I do not really know more than that about what happens to them, but the light does transmute all that darkness. And for me there is the added benefit of the vibrations in the room changing from heavy and dark to lighter and peaceful.

My gracious husband over the decades naturally got used to this kind of thing. Eventually he could recognize the difference in energy in the places where it was disturbed or heavy. He will leave a place because he does not want to be around that heavy, unpleasant energy. Or on other occasions he asks me to send it away.

This was a first though: him coming to me in a dream and asking me to clear the entities from his energy field. He did not even have to wake up to deal with them. Ha!

Part 3:
Growing in Awareness

Chapter 9
Peace without Effort

I own who I am. I own my goodness, my greatness and am rarely appalled by my humanness. With less judgement, I clean the house or don't. I do not even evaluate my shopping and eating (previous areas of addictive behavior) as good or bad. It just was. The key is doing the work to free me of strong opinions, and freeing me from functioning from need. Then living, doing the basics, such as providing myself the foods my body prefers, not judging food, actions or me.

Internally, I hear and know things about people that I only bring to their attention if they want the information. I receive and share as my inner senses and awareness direct me. This helps clients, students and friends see what they now are ready to know and to change if they choose.

My confidence has moved beyond where it once was. Once, I could only claim I am a great reading teacher. My greatness stopped there. Now I know I am a great human being, while not better than anyone. Undeniably, all of us hold in our essence, the greatness of infinite Source.

Peace returns without effort, I look within, stop listening to the chatter in my head and immediately have peace. There is a quiet place always available. Moving my attention there I sense my connection with something greater than myself, move into awareness and enjoy the calm.

Earlier this year, I got caught up in the drama of my nineteen year old kitty, Scout showing symptoms of serious illness. Was he dying? I took him to the vet and cried before she even saw him. Yes, I was sad I might lose my cat. Not sad he might die. No, he lived a great life; getting to chase bunnies and field mice; outliving his sister and many cats that had lived with us, getting to sleep on our bed, coming and sitting on us while we watched television switching from one lap to the other to get petted, petted and petted. Oh, what a life. Getting canned food when it appeared dry food was not meeting his needs, plus getting filtered water so fewer toxins entered his little body. Getting stairs made beside the bed so he could climb up once his arthritis made jumping up and down painful. Yep, a good life.

Then I realized while I stood in the veterinarian's office, that this was me planning a familiar grieving response to the possibility of losing a beloved cat. My cat, Scout gets to come and go in life and death as suits him. He will transition to energy. In my infinite self, I am aware of the perfection of it. In my Lynne body with restricted awareness, I grieve.

Well, actually after that visit, Scout came home with a few medications and lived even longer. He probably had cancer so we did not know how long he would be with us. His choice. We kept him as comfortable as possible. I knew I probably would cry again. I preferred, however, to view it from that other perspective where he is perfection and to focus on gratitude for what we had, knowing we will know each other intimately again.

When his illness progressed so the simple act of walking appeared difficult, we had the traveling vet come over. Scout now rests under the lemon tree in our back yard. His passing at what felt like the right time caused much less grief than I expected or felt with previous kitties passing.

My goal is to reach a point that when triggers arise, I do not react to them. That I recognize them as triggers and am only reminded of a previous time of reactivity that is irrelevant today.

Today my inner peace is almost unshakeable. I feel grateful however, that I recognize and respond to the triggers quickly with laughter or the willingness to allow everything and everyone to be just as they are.

Chapter 10
Expanding Understanding

I have written in my previous books how I thought much of what happened in my relationship with my mother showed a lack of love on her part. My understanding changed in my fifties as my acceptance grew; I could see the gift in what I felt was her emotional abandonment of me. She loved me.

She struggled with her own existence, with abuse and with the death of two daughters and a husband. I thought she distanced herself from me. Maybe she did.

At the same time, because my family provided religious exposure for me as a child I knew that something extremely powerful existed in the world and if I could find it, it would give me the love I craved. In response to growing up with a feeling of loneliness and emptiness, I was propelled to look for God. I had concluded early in life people can be there for you sometimes, yet were unable to be there for me to the extent I wanted.

Similarly I suspected my mom did not get enough comfort from her faith. Her faith and yet continued suffering conflicted with what I had been taught. This too caused me to seek and investigate other ways of thinking. I eventually found Buddhism which explained life's ups and downs much better for me.

My mother's struggles and imperfections held hidden gifts for me. I seized the benefits and continued forward to create a belief system and way of life that worked well for me. Her gift of intelligence, her expectation that I would go to college, her faith in me all helped me to be all that I could be. Her traits, my traits, our shared experiences combined and forged me into the being I am, strong, intelligent, compassionate and curious. There were decades I could not see what to be thankful for in our experiences, but that is one of the gifts of time and a spiritual practice; perspective changes everything.

Doesn't everyone seem to have "mother issues" to deal with? It appears that way to me. For one friend, it was her mother's narcissism, for another the mother's food and shopping addiction, for another that her mother did not protect her and one whose mother was diagnosed with bipolar disorder. A woman brought down the house during a group discussion in a meeting I attended by stating, "If it isn't one thing, it's your mother"!

As a teenager, I dismissed the traditional churches I'd been taken to a child – Methodist, Catholic, Presbyterian, and Nazarene and decided I would study other religions. Gradually I pieced together a faith that worked for me. In this process I trusted there was something omnipotent that would help me. I built faith because of the evidence I received over the years that yes, there is something amazing, beautiful, loving, and gentle while powerful that knows me and cares about every aspect of me. My understanding of that force has deepened to where I know now that it is not something outside of me to seek but is that force that created me that I am still part of and can always touch when I am still.

As I continued to study enlightened teachers, I found the guidance I sought. My understanding is once again being stretched. I am now reading Sri Nisargadetta Maharaj and see that he says knowing I Am That as myself is necessary in the process of full realization, but it is not full realization; it's just on the path.

Full realization has to do with not seeing us as separate beings but as something greater or even as part of something greater. So all the teachings I have followed that assert "Seek God", imply that God is outside me. Better are those that tell us "Seek God inside you." Now I know I am infinite and my consciousness identified as Lynne is only one part of me. While incarnated here, I have thought of me as something separate, an individual. But it is a perception, not a truth.

I am consciousness – sometimes in a body, sometimes not. I am on a path to see through the incarnations and the constructs of time, space and the collective consciousness to fully realize myself. In this life, I strive to know Truth while in body to the degree that I know Truth when I am in full awareness of myself as God in the in-between times.

Chapter 11
Gurus, Teachers and Masters

For decades, I thought others had the answers and I needed them to help me. I felt undefined and uncertain back then. The wise spiritual teachers and authors who have gone before us lit the way for me, opening doors, changing my understanding, bringing me resources, offering support and love. Some I appreciated. Some I didn't notice. Now I appreciate even the one I did not particularly like.

One outcome in thinking others had what I needed was having one teacher in my life for more than fifteen years. From that one teacher I received the wisdom I was ready for but also a great deal of criticism. My responsibility in the situation lay in my willingness to be criticized. It took fifteen years for me to say enough is enough.

Around that time I connected with another spiritual teacher for ten years, during which we talked almost every day. She helped me let go of a lot of pain and shame, and taught me to check my motives and to journal regularly.

For twenty-five years, I met regularly (a minimum of once a week) with a large spiritual fellowship. In those meetings, I heard God speak to me directly through the others there. They said exactly what I needed to hear. Regularly I heard a piece of timely information for my journey. These people functioned as teachers too although generally unknowingly.

There are teachers in spirit besides those in the physical. Anytime I want to grow in an area I ask God to send me a teacher who can help me with that area of my life. Just as an aside, I also ask that I am open and willing to get what I need, to learn quickly and easily so it doesn't come down to getting the two by four upside my head to get my attention due to my stubbornness.

I think the spiritual teachers, the guides, angels, and masters work with us all day and all night. All we have to do is ask. They come, assist us, then go when they are finished.

Today in meditation I asked for additional clarity and psychic ability. Although unfamiliar to me up until that time, Archangel Raziel came to me. I heard his name and paused to look up information about him. His presence precisely addressed my request for clarity and an increase in seeing, hearing and knowing. According to Doreen Virtue's *Archangels and Ascended Masters* book, he is an archangel of clairvoyance and spiritual understanding. He also is subtle, loving, kind and intelligent and helps us when asked.

I think the point is ask. There are so many beings, angels, guardians and highly evolved beings that want to help. All we have to do is ask and receive.

Although some teachings state that you must commit yourself to a guru and dedicate your whole life to them. That was appropriate for some at an earlier time. It is not so relevant anymore. At least, in my life it appears so. You can change teachers when ready. Often we grow and then attract someone who can guide us to a new level. Be discerning. Let your higher-self guide you.

At times, I considered how wonderful it sounded having a guru, a master like they do in Hinduism and Buddhism. Having someone I could put all my trust in and would lead me to enlightenment. That path sounded great and still it was not for me. It is, however, perfect for those who choose it.

Gurus can facilitate us while in spirit too. Possibly I have not chosen one on Earth because I have Babaji and Jesus on the other side guiding me.

Even as I remained open to new awareness and growth perpetuated by others I changed and became a spiritual teacher for others too. I am a dedicated student and a joyful teacher, the facilitator of personal and spiritual growth.

Chapter 12
Magical

The number of magical healing modalities available today is remarkable. Throughout this book I share my favorites and how I have used them.

In Access Consciousness Bars® class, we learn to release old patterns through a clearing statement. First, we trigger all the emotions that comes up around an issue. Then we use the Access Consciousness clearing statement to clear it. Afterwards, we are lighter, less encumbered, although it feels unfamiliar. The first time I experienced the clearing statement and Access Bars I felt uncomfortable afterwards because I felt so different. In no time at all, I adjusted, feeling less burdened. As always I feel enthusiastic about getting rid of the limiting stuff. I end up trusting this modality because I saw how effective "running the Bars" and using the clearing statement are.

Then on top of that I noticed the resulting emptiness – part of the enlightenment process in Buddhism. The clearing statement was removing stuff for me that I did not have to carry any more and I got more emptiness in return (to be clear, not a negative like loneliness) simply more spacious inside.

Healing myself through writing, through talk, through counseling, through teachings, or processes like Access Bars and ThetaHealing creates a sense a freedom, a sense of ease in life. For others, it appears to be more a sense of relief that they aren't burdened by the worries, resentment and cares that troubled them before the session.

These modalities appear magical, quite different and more effective than when I counseled clients in a drug and alcohol treatment center. That was good stuff, but slow and the relapse rate still was too high. My clients today do not usually have substance problems. They do come to me with resentments, anger, and fear, questions about their jobs, their relationships, and the future. Often they want change but are a bit reluctant because change brings the unknown and that is considered scary stuff.

With private clients today I never tell them what to do even if they ask me directly. Instead, magical things happen. For example, a client clearly shifted gears and decided to leave her marriage. She had pondered it for over a year. Once she made the decision in the session, messages came for her about financial security, steps of preparation, where to find emotional support, how to prepare for those who won't understand her decision and on and on. The information comes easily through Spirit, the client finds clarity and leaves with the certainty they are moving forward on the right track.

Magical because when I teach ThetaHealing classes, students who had never considered themselves healers before become healers and advance quickly. Students who have never done a reading before learn how to connect with the highest source and give a reading. People start seeing angels, guides and other beings. They get a little blown away by their abilities. Still the desire to go forward carries them as they learn and grow.

Magical because I now can pause at any time and ask and get answers. What joy it brings that the sense of "knowing" is easier and easier to reach. The boundaries between me and my true self are falling away.

We actually exist without limits. We exude potential. Each one of us is different, unique in how we'll manifest our

Unfolding the Mystery of Self

potential, in how we see it in ourselves or how others will see or not see it in us. Without limits, we live in awareness, not even stopping to pause by having to access knowing.

Also magical, always being in the state of connectedness, always realizing I am surrounded by beings without form. Frankly not seeing them with our physical eyes means little. They are still there. Angels, teachers, guides, leprechauns, gnomes, bad ass demons, and fairies; all vibrantly alive. We were taught to dismiss such things as unreal when we saw them as children. Most of us came to believe they did not exist.

Here's my favorite troll story. I was at a family reunion in Oregon and walking on a dirt road with three of my uncles. As we strolled along and talked, I must have gasped because they asked what was wrong. I told them I had seen a troll leaning against a tree ahead of us on the right. They said let's keep walking and we did. I was stunned by the sight and they avoided discussing it any further. Even without validation, it was a spectacular, unforgettable moment for me.

Mostly I live in a mystical, connected state and yet I can get uncertain on occasion or still identify myself as what I do; being a college professor or identifying myself by how I felt so much of my earlier life as a "wall flower" or "less than". Those moments, those feelings quickly pass now.

Most of the time I live more in the joy of being me. I may not be fully familiar with the new me that is emerging, still I do like challenges and knowing I am growing. In fact, there is no boring here, just one new thing after another. What used to be: I had a traumatic early life and consequently would easily come to tears. I attracted friends who wanted to limit me and judge me. As Eleanor Roosevelt declared, "No one can make you feel inferior without your consent."

Despite all that now I find myself intuitive, loving, sensitive, empowered, spiritual, capable and creative. These traits were always in me just waiting to blossom. Much of what I consider magical actually includes the daily work of personal growth, a spiritual practice and determination. The grace within us and all the factors already mentioned bring inner peace, change and gratitude.

Chapter 13
No Mistakes

As we grow in awareness, we "see" and "know" more. When ready more advanced teachers are available whether in spirit, in person or through the internet. We do not have to go to India and find a guru or swami. Yoga is available at the YMCA. Meditation is available at the spa. You can study Christianity, Buddhism, Zoroastrianism, Judaism, or create your own path by choosing what suits you. The only trick is having sufficient awareness to recognize and avoid the charlatans, the teachers with extreme egos and power trips. If your gut says the teacher is iffy, walk away.

Although sometimes we stick with a spiritual teacher to learn more than the spiritual teaching; maybe we have karma with the person: maybe we unknowingly must replay our family's dysfunction with the teacher or choose a teacher as parent figure. That is OK too. Learn from them, from yourself and the situation. Part of what you might learn is what you do *not* want. Then you can walk away when you are done knowing you learned and grew.

Experiencing struggle with a spiritual teacher reminds me that we do not make mistakes. Thinking we made a mistake is actually misunderstanding. Everything and everyone in our lives present opportunity for growth. All that we have judged ourselves for as wrong really means a misinterpretation of the circumstance.

My high school friend, Lisa once asked me to channel for her back in the 80s. She was told by the one who spoke with her through me that she judged herself too harshly. That all she thought she had done wrong – for instance having a child while unmarried, or giving it up for adoption actually were perfect experiences; all very valuable to her. The number of mistakes she'd made was tiny compared to what she thought. If she could see herself as the energy of a being who came here to learn and grow through experience she might accept the wondrous being she truly is.

At that time, the message she received that day surprised me because I did not know back then that all of our choices and experiences are really perfection, allowing us to have great diversity of experience. Through trial-and-error we find our way to what we do want, to what does make us happy. Along the way we develop courage, humility and perseverance to name a few of the virtues we develop in each life.

Lack of perspective on events, judging myself as wrong and as having made big mistakes, all evidenced themselves in this situation: I married at the age of seventeen and divorced at nineteen. I felt terrible about the divorce, even badly about marrying so young. I judged myself as bad, sad and wrong. Yet I looked back years later and knew the perfection in marrying young as a means to become independent of my parents and family alcoholism and violence. After a few more years passed, I even realized the perfection of the divorce which set me free to move into the next stages of my life. Now I think of my ex, Bill, with gratitude for his part in all that. Our actions were not mistakes. They were valuable opportunities and experiences.

Funny, how what we think is all wrong about us may only be misinterpretation. Given time or distance we see more clearly and might realize no mistakes were made.

Chapter 14
In This Lifetime

In this very special time period, we live with the great potential for self-realization, for enlightenment. The Earth's energies, with new higher vibrations accelerating, make it easier for all of us. In conjunction, many children born today (called crystal children) are more open and aware as have been the rainbow, indigo, bronze and gold children over the past sixty years.

The energy of life today makes some of the previous traditional spiritual teachings less relevant because everything is progressing much faster.

Thank goodness because when I read the Buddhist view on what it takes to reach enlightenment and the many traps, the many ways to get lost, and to fall back, it scared and discouraged me. They explain even the possibility of getting stuck in nothingness or in bliss for ages never reaching full enlightenment. Scary stuff.

I know I have come so close in other lives, that I lived on the mountaintop several times, lived in bliss and was unable to care for my own body. I was of little use to anyone. Possibly living with the high vibrations of bliss raised the vibrations of those who came near my body. That is not enough for me. Not this lifetime: I lived in bliss, now I want enlightenment, along with engagement with people. The Buddhist mind for enlightenment means that as we generate a mind for full awakening we do so for the benefit of all sentient beings.

Several sources have told me in this lifetime I will achieve full self-realization. I'm grateful for that and will do so while living and working in the world, not just for myself but for all beings still suffering.

Fortunately, in this time period new possibilities exist. As a result, intuition appears not only to be increasing, but apparent in people who might have rejected it as unreal before. For example, more and more people acknowledge sensing deceased loved ones visiting and offering love and comfort.

It appears that after 2012 things really did change - not as the so- called end-of-the-world as a few predicted, but with the positives that many never heard about so did not know to expect.

Remember the music of the 1960's hinting of what was to come?

- o The Time Has Come
- o Age of Aquarius
- o Crystal Blue Persuasion

Not only were they saying things needed to change; they also suggested we were already headed into a special time. Some knew and sang of it for us back then.

One way to describe how I see these changes is living now in the state of allowing - no judgments of self or others. Allowing my old friend to be as critical as she is, and not spending as much time with her as I used to. Allowing my newer friend to be as mean as she is and again spending less time with her while letting go of judgement of her.

Allowing my wonderful husband to be who he is; gorgeous, lovable, big, and strong and still wearing colors, patterns and fabrics like a blind person. He is also bright and fun and allows me to be overweight, sensitive, odd, peaceful, and loving without judgment.

I could think of this world as a mess - most people evil, aliens as conspirators planning to destroy us - or I can allow the world to be what it is, people what they are, aliens what they are. The only thinking that sounds appealing now besides allowing is setting intention, noticing beauty and love. I choose to ignore the conspiracy theories. Life flows with ease.

Most of the time, I am in a state of allowing and going with the flow. When my neck hurts, I pause, and breathe deep knowing the discomfort will pass. I allow it to pass. My shoulder hurts. I ask myself whose pain is it. Not mine, I realize, and release it. The state of allowing relaxes, brings ease and more of my true self appears. Recognizing what is mine and what I picked up from others is key here. As empaths we pick up thoughts, illness, and energy from everyone around us and must learn to distinguish what is ours and what isn't. Then life becomes much easier.

In the state of allowing I release encumbrances, I hear my inner voice better, knowing comes faster, and very importantly I am much less likely to judge myself. Another form of allowing appears when I am out running errands. It is a sense of being in the flow, knowing in which order to do the errands, knowing what first, what is beyond my limits for the day. Flow, timeliness and ease show me my connectivity with Source. All considered by the new age/spiritual communities as part of humanity's long awaited evolution.

Allowing includes feeling the flow when the words come out on paper (or into the computer) without editing; they come rapidly one after the other. I more easily recognize when I am in the right place, right time, which validates the effortlessness of "being in the flow." Flow becomes apparent on a grander scale for me when I look back over time and realize oh, I was there and met that person, I was there and helped the dog get back to his home and was in the flow to open the door to the next right kitty.

Accepting the times when I am not in the flow, when I am out of sorts or surprised because life feels like a struggle, these are usually times of transition or the lulls between growth spurts. Does anyone enjoy that time? Usually a sense of wanting, or a vague unhappiness is pervasive. People sound pretty uncomfortable when they are in it. Generally we lose perspective as we step into a low period or into chaos before going into a growth spurt.

For me, besides annoyance there might be fear, because standing still is frightening. Again all phases of life exist perfectly as they are. Only our lack of perspective deems it not so.

Chapter 15
So Many Lives

The drama of reincarnation; for how many billions of years and how many thousands of lives? We jump into physical life (bodies) again and again. We embrace experience, reject experience and gain experience. How many lives? I remember too many to recount, but then again I have been told I will eventually remember them all. I listed some of mine that easily come to mind. Probably anyone who spent time considering their past lives could easily create their own list if it mattered.

Places I remember include foreign cities and countries: Venice, Rome, Italy's mountainous region, Malta, a Philippine island, Russia, Atlantis, Israel's caves, Egypt, Norway, the west coast of South America, the South coast of France and Atlantis.

In the United States I remember South Carolina, Virginia, Alaska, St. Louis, San Francisco, Virginia City, plus the southern states and the Navajo Lands.

The other memories I cannot attribute to Earth: a sparsely populated planet, an underwater city, and a planet with two moons.

It may even be possible to remember those times between lives, times without form. My friend, Tara Brown, a multimodality healer/practitioner, says I already have had more than 100,000 lives. Who knew? She even provided detail, for instance that I knew Sunny, my friend Betty's dog, in sixty-seven lives. How amusing and is it possibly so? Then again was it life with Sunny as a dog or in other forms? I only have seen maybe three lives with him and they were all joyful.

I think the large number of lives we live includes the assignments between lives such as when we are a guide or a teacher for someone else. It includes life on other planets. Does it include life in other dimensions? Probably.

In truth, the evolutionary process for me includes gradually remembering these lives on occasion finding myself amazed and excited with the information. On the other hand, they are examples of incarnations. It is not who we are, it is what we have been and done.

Chapter 16
Concurrently

As I wrote this book I sensed others present; nonphysical beings around me. I asked, "How many beings are here with me right now?" I heard seventeen, comprised of angels and masters. I also received the understanding they illuminate me in my work while at the same time, they are me! Then, I noticed their delight at my awareness of them; some clapped, and others laughed. Connecting with them made the writing of this book even easier.

The seventeen with me as I write I call a cadre. They said they are intergalactic and multidimensional and here with me while existing concurrently and working on other planes. It reminded me how Richard Bach nailed it when he wrote in his books that all lives, all time, exists concurrently. We think of our lives as linear; like we think of time as linear. How can Atlantis, the dark ages, World War II and today all take place at the same time? Expanding our knowing beyond the constructs of time and space, we begin to understand.

Part of the picture that comes from considering your many lives includes recognizing your soul family. Their vibrations are similar to yours. Some still live in drama unaware how to break free. Some are fully free. They are your soul-self-expressed in a myriad of ways. In my case, the first two soul family members I recognized were Daniel, a radiant spiritual teacher challenged by his great awareness while living in an ordinary city with ordinary people. Also Kathleen, an aspirant of a spiritual life burdened by low self-esteem and compulsive collecting. As I spent time getting to know them in this life, I recognized them as part of me. Probably I easily recognized them because they were closer in origin to me within the soul family. Tara also tells me there are more than 2,700 in my soul group. Much larger than I would have guessed.

We are in this place and time while we are in all the others, too. It all occurs concurrently. Everything occurs in the "now" moment. All past and future are in the present moment. Time is an illusion constructed because of the density of life in the physical and because of the laws governing this plane. The physical (from a body to the universes), and the divisions between planes of existence, are just ultimately constructs necessary and useful for our comprehension of life. The small part of ourselves that incarnates each time required it to be so.

Here is one way it was shown to me to help me understand it. Envision a meadow, green, wide, long, and radiant with life. In that meadow are 700 billion blades of grass. You can identify yourself as the meadow or as a single blade of grass. You exist as both. You can expand your awareness to know yourself as both when you put your attention on each and expand your perspective like the analogy with the child in chapter seven. Try sitting with the image of yourself as the meadow. Then add knowing you are so infinite that you include and are connected with all the blades of grass.

Have you read the book *Initiation* by Elisabeth Haich? In it she gives an example, using a cube, to show that perspective is the only limitation. Expand your awareness out and instead of seeing a single spot on the cube because your nose is up against it, back up and you can see the cube as a large wall. Or move back further and look for a corner point, then you see three sides at once. Unfortunately most of us cannot see all six sides of the cube yet. Perspective changes everything.

We mostly see ourselves as separate blades of grass while we actually are much more. The life force in us is in all the grass, and in all life. We are the same thing. This concept of being the blade or the meadow is still more linear and singular than life, than the energy that we are in totality.

You are creator; early on you created multiple versions of you, some you recognize as lives, some you recognize as soul family, some you have not recognized yet. Some of the energy that you are, is in the space of possibility and not yet ever physical. All are you. Cool!

Chapter 17
Teaching

Discussing my book *Living Hope – Steps to Leaving Suffering Behind* in my "spiritual topics" book club led to two surprising responses. First, I concluded I must more carefully choose my words after I shocked one woman who is a new Buddhist when I told her there is a state of awareness beyond living within the confines of the Law of Cause and Effect. She couldn't imagine it. She had discovered karma and was excited that it was everything. Next time I may prefer to assess the person's preparedness before I share my less common-place contemplations.

In *Living Hope*, I give detailed definitions and explanations of cause and effect in our lives and about my process of coming to terms with the events in my life within the context of karma. I more recently have considered that some people have transcended the Law of Cause and Effect. There are people who have balanced karma for others intentionally with an action, described in the *New Testament Bible* in the life of Jesus Christ, and by Baba Ram Dass's experiences with his Maharaj in *Be Here Now*, and more recently through Prana Deeksha (a blessing and healing process) as taught at Oneness University in India.

There are those who reached self-realization who no longer create karma (at least not the problematic kind) for themselves. In my early thirties, I realized I had reached the point of completing my dramatic past life karma. I have met a few people who also believe they live in this space.

I am aware of more and more people who have finished with karma. Yet that is enough to give me food for thought. Might I entertain the possibility of creating my life with a potency and awareness and oneness that I might live beyond cause and effect? Hmmm. Masters and Gurus lived as examples of transcendence while remaining in body. How long does it take? What does it look like? What is possible for the non-Guru? Who else might I study?

The second eye-opening conversation in book club that morning occurred when another woman appeared uncomfortable during the discussion of the Law of Cause and Effect. She objected to the implications of her responsibility for the events and people in her life. I wanted that conversation to slow down. I could barely respond to one question before the next one came. Fortunately, as we acknowledged the magnitude of the topic, she expressed interest in studying further until it makes sense to her. Resolving the questions of "Why bad things happen in my life?" and "How could I have any responsibility for it?" requires deep consideration. It took me years to come to peace with my responsibly in creating this life for myself.

Is it possible what I consider a challenging discussion is actually perfection because everyone present had their awareness expanded somewhat that morning over coffee and banana bread?

Part 4:
Healing

Chapter 18
Healing Tools

Healing work includes healing physically, mentally, emotionally and spiritually. God/Creator/Source/the Divine/ heals, not me. I have not that power.

I do have tools, training, sensitivity and the ability to pay attention, to recognize when it is time to tune in, to hear and to use those tools. I learned to be guided and to let the energy flow through or when appropriate to switch on the natural healing ability in the client's body. I know to listen, be intuitive, to pray and to be present. All of that goes into the process. At the same time, I know there is always more I will learn.

When to heal?

- When asked to or when your intuition tells you it's a good time to offer. Recently a friend was distraught so I offered and he took me up on it. Issues that caused his discomfort became apparent, were cleared and gave him relief. He called later that day to thank me and reported he hadn't been aware that betrayal was at the base of his distress and was grateful to realize it as part of ongoing issues with female figures in his life.
- As a healer our social norms can slow us down. To speak up to strangers when I sense they are ill, to offer a healing when they didn't ask for help doesn't feel

right. I usually say nothing and go through a process of internally asking for guidance – asking, "Do I say something?" I wait for a sign. If nothing happens telling me to speak up, I figure the silence is divine guidance too.
- On a few occasions I have offered before being asked. Once there was a hairdresser in a salon who had been doing a cleanse for her health and felt terrible when she came to work. I was there getting my hair cut. I offered her a healing, she said yes, I held her hand and silently prayed. It was over in a minute. We chatted briefly. She said she felt better. I finished up with my hairdresser and went on my way. It is deeply satisfying when I offer, the person accepts and it goes well.
- When not to heal: Sometimes I get a message a person is ill solely because I am intuitive, not because I am supposed to do or say anything.

How to heal?

- I use the tools I have learned that include ThetaHealing, color therapy, Access Bars, Access Consciousness body work, Reiki, chakra Balancing, Golden Orb Deeksha, general energy work and more. Personally I intend to continue to study and expand my work and understanding. Two of these healing modalities did not exist twenty-five years ago. Who knows what is next? *At the end of this chapter I have provided a definition for each of the terms.
- Why use traditional medical care? For me only when healing techniques won't solve it after trying multiple times. In truth, energetic healing can repair a broken

bone immediately, right in front of your eyes. Allow that.
- There are many, many more tools; here are few more – massage, acupuncture, shamanistic practices, aromatherapy, Ayurveda, yoga and Rolfing. You have to use your own intuition as to what is right for you, of what you might want to learn and offer the world.
- You can heal with your hands (still energy work) in person or heal long distance.
- Sometimes you have to ask clients to lower their barriers and open themselves to receive more.

How does it work?

- It works because of the natural positive nature of the universe, of Creator. Life is set up this way. Most healing modalities bring in life-force energy called chi, qi, ki, and/or prana, depending on the language. We can direct it or activate it to work on behalf of the one in need. We can accelerate it or direct it with tools, with crystals, and with specific prayers.
- It has been possible to heal ailments slowly – repeated healings on my friend's toe (fungus) made progress until I stopped doing it and the fungus took over again. That situation was a good example of a person who didn't do the internal work (belief work) so he recreated the same health problem. With my sick nineteen-year-old kitty when I offered him healing, his eyes cleared and his ability to hear remained strong, while his arthritis never improved that I could discern.
- For myself, I had prayed to heal the eye condition I was diagnosed with called Fuchs Dystrophy. I worked on it a few times with some improvement. Not until I prayed

for a DNA change from Fuchs dystrophy to perfect form and function did I get results. The last time I went to the eye doctor he said you barely have any indication of Fuchs, don't worry about it. So I don't.
- Some things heal immediately like my friend's chemically induced headache. She had just gotten a vaccination and had a headache for hours. It cleared immediately with ThetaHealing.
- By the way, with most healing work, the healer energetically receives a healing at the same time as the person getting the healing. With Access Bars or Access Consciousness body work the healers receive a healing of any issues they have related to what the client releases.

Healing works because of several factors:

1. Creator does the work
2. The healer is a vehicle
   a. Willingness of both healer and client is necessary
   b. High vibrations matter
   c. None of the illness stays in the healer's body
   d. Tools (modalities) help
   e. Being aware/listening to inner guidance
3. People must be ready to release the illness
   a. Determine if the illness serves a purpose for the person
   b. Sometimes belief work must be done before a healing can be received
   c. It is beneficial for the ill person to know why they created the illness and how it served him/her.

*Definitions of terms:

ThetaHealing®: created by Vianna Stibal. Using the Theta and Delta brain wave state, along with connection with Creator then healing is requested. At that point, Creator makes instantaneous changes in physical, emotional, spiritual and mental well-being. Through intuition limiting beliefs are identified, then through focused prayer they are cleared also positive thoughts and virtues are added.

Color therapy: simply focusing on healing colors and sending energy of that color to the injured area or to the person as a whole. Green is used most often (but never for cancer), blue to counter pain and white for the highest vibration.

Access Bars®: is the touching of 32 points on the head – called having your Bars run. It is a nurturing and relaxing treatment used to facilitate change in all areas of life. Bars slows down the brain waves allowing behavior patterns, belief systems, limitations and points of view from childhood and other lifetimes to be released. This modality literally changes the probabilities of one's future.

Access Consciousness body work: involves using any of the many process as requested by the body. It includes for example, a hands-on-healing process to release trauma from the body. It helps with unresolved pain, restriction of motion, repeated trauma and repetitive stress disorders.

Reiki: a form of alternative medicine developed in 1922 by Japanese Buddhist Mikao Usui has been adapted into varying cultural traditions across the world. Reiki practitioners use *hands-on healing* by which chi – universal life force is transferred through the palms of the practitioner to a patient in order to encourage healing.

Chakra balancing: is the Yogic practice of attending to each of the seven energy points (considered the most important of the chakras) in the subtle body that run from the crown of the head to the base of the spine. By sending prana energy each chakra is balanced, cleansed, opened until bright and rotating clockwise which leads to health and balance spiritually, physically, mentally, and emotionally.

Golden Orb Deeksha: taught by Oneness University, this blessing is the giving of Golden energy from a person who has received it (and trained with it) to another. The purpose is to awaken in us the experience of Oneness. Sourced in the Divine it operates appropriately in response to the needs of the individual and initiates neurobiological change in the brain. It is accompanied with spontaneous feelings of joy, calm and connection to Oneness. It leads to one's own awakening.

More information on each healing modality can be found in the internet and the library.

Chapter 19
Healing Self

In order to be an effective healer, we must first heal ourselves (if not completely, at least begin); similar to how counselors and therapists in-training are required to first receive counseling in the process of earning a degree. For healers, it is less formalized. Before certified, licensed or given a degree, counselors are required to attend counseling groups and to be supervised by their professors who usually are licensed or certified counselor supervisors. As we work through our own issues we get clearer and are less likely to mistake our own issue as the client's issue, therefore less likely to project our insecurity, anger, fear and mommy or daddy issues on to the patient or client; as important for us in alternative healing as it is for counselors, therapists, psychologists and psychiatrists.

While sick with the flu recently, I discovered that even when the body feels sick, at the same time, I am consciousness, have joy, and find life fun. My consciousness is not sick. That awareness was a delightful confirmation that we are not our bodies. They are ours and we actually are more than that. Our consciousness is formless and pain free.

Currently I am considering how some of my client's interests parallel mine. Sometimes as I engage in a session with a client I will notice recurring themes of sacrifice, of fear and the very common "I am not enough" belief. It is most striking when the subject the client is addressing is one that has been on my mind too. Is it because we are one thing (not separate) at the core? Is it because I can only talk about what I know and not someone else reality? Or are these universal themes?

For example, I read that when Baba Ram Dass was a psychotherapist, he noticed his clients paralleled his own self-worth issues. So most likely these are universal themes.

In our healing work, service and helping are not codependent, although they can be when one's life is compelled by the past. I released with ThetaHealing the program I have to be of service, just like I released the need to sacrifice myself. I *choose* to be of service and to help others because it is easy, because I care, and because I have so much to give. Most of all doing healing work is fun. Assisting and observing as clients address emotional suffering and move to a more peaceful state is particularly satisfying.

I can lift up my brother, to whatever level he wishes and can love my sister (metaphorically speaking) until she can love herself. I give service because I can. I have enough for myself. I enjoy imparting all that is available to others.

It remains very important for me to continuously be aware of my work with others and understand the potential complications of projection, transference, countertransference and other confusion that may arise when delving into people's health and lives. I aspire to constantly be aware of my continuing personal growth, watching for triggers, old patterns and clearing out that which is incompatible with a spiritual life.

Chapter 20
Healers

Fear can stop healers from fully developing their gifts. Most healers have programming to some degree which causes them to believe healers are harmed or killed for being healers which then prevents them from opening themselves to learn and progress.

Throughout history, healers were tortured, were sent away to obscurity and/or were killed. Due to their personal experiences and the atrocities observed over their lifetimes these beliefs/programs became locked into place.

In the past, I too feared I could be noticed, caught, discredited, tortured, and/or killed. Lots of people in metaphysical classes and healing classes, find themselves stuck or afraid to move forward because of the kinds of body and soul memories I am describing. All these events, these travesties, were common in earlier time periods; however in the present time often the memories remain at a subconscious level. Often the person decides or promises themselves they will never do that work again.

Part of my fear arose from at least one past life. For example, in one I was held in the community stocks until I died for being my powerful self who helped, who healed, had insight, and talked to God. I suspect it happened many times, with different details that I have not yet remembered. Today, as I step back into clairvoyance, clairsentience and healing abilities means feeling vulnerable. At least, it seemed that way at first. That is not to say I was a healer in every life. I also lived lives as a slave ship employee, a leper, a singer, a young virgin sacrifice, a leader of cult of women devotees, a soldier who raped and pillaged after winning battles. So, no, not always a healer.

Fortunately in these times, we do not consider healers to be witches and burn them at the stake anymore, at least not in this country. Thank goodness. Although, I still notice strange looks if my healing work or psychic awareness comes up at a dinner party or an environmental event.

It is likely if a person is interested in being a healer today, they have been healers many times in past lives. If they have suffered from persecution as a healer, blocks will show up for them. However, these can be cleared, freeing the healer to proceed with grace and ease.

Most people who believe in reincarnation agree it appears we have all lived thousands of lives. We have seen all, been all, done all - good and bad. That is about free will and experiencing ourselves in a myriad of ways in the density of the physical. Clearing and empowering self as a healer entails releasing all the wounds from the lives, freeing ourselves of the fear, the adamantly declared, "I'll never put myself in that position again." So the oaths and vows can be cleared too, freeing us up to heal using any of the modalities that fit for us.

Chapter 21
Feeling Their Pain

When I am out in public, there is a part of me that occasionally senses people who are in pain or ill. Then an inherent desire kicks up in me to touch or be with them to take away the pain or the problem.

Empaths' bodies want to take on others' illnesses, even a stranger's pain or disease, because we know we can heal it. I ask my body to not do much of that. I like to be alerted of important information so I can help my clients. Never do I like to have my body absorb illness without my awareness. When I realize I have taken on an illness, I undo it. Unfortunately I stored other people's stuff in my body for decades before I realized my body did that. Yuck.

Taking on peoples stuff is unhealthy. At one writing conference, while working in a room with about fifty people in it, I felt a great amount of tension and a sense of pressure. It was not my tension. Still, I felt it in my body and thought it was mine for a while. To rid myself of the habit of taking on people's problems unconsciously and thinking the discomfort and pains are mine takes continuous awareness. It takes remembering I am Spirit, an unlimited being - in a body.

When in a public place picking up on someone's pain or illness I can use my awareness to let it pass through me, acknowledge it and let it go. Awareness means noticing what goes on and doing nothing unless asked, compelled or guided.

While working with clients, I occasionally feel in my body some kind of discomfort, usually symbolizing an important issue for them. For example, once when working with a female client my heart started hurting, I asked the client what was going on with her heart. After pinpointing it like that for her, she opened up and talked about the pain of her childhood experience. We went on to heal her grief regarding her parents and one grandparent. In another session with a different client, I felt discomfort in my stomach and asked the client about it, saying it appeared connected to betrayal. She explained some of the betrayal she experienced as a child and we proceeded to heal some of that. In those cases, my body provided accurate and valuable information which helps me and helps my clients. As soon as the client begins to release the triggering issue the discomfort in my body disappears.

Interestingly I find some of my clients, especially the ascended master types take on other's stuff too. I've observed they take on their parents' guilt, shame, anger in order to help their parents. It does not actually help. It does affect the child. But then a child doesn't realize the futility in it, they do it out of love. Often part of clients moving forward involves releasing the parents or the ancestor's pattern of emotion, poverty, sacrifice and/or other limiting programs in order to heal. Life with freedom of choice instead of compelled by genetic programming is much easier after the release.

Chapter 22
Healing with a Touch

Healing – mmm, that word makes me feel good. I love healing myself and others and not only physical healing. It brings deep satisfaction to talk with a person and help them release what does not serve them anymore. With ThetaHealing I identify the limiting beliefs they can release then pray for that change. After entering a session feeling burdened or unhappy, the client then transitions as we work and lightens up in an hour. The client often has an "aha" moment, is blissful or in a relaxed state, then talks as if the problem wasn't even there; the problem becomes more like a memory. He or she asks for change and it comes.

Although healing myself, others, pets, even trees, started back in my twenties, I'm still in awe each time. Today thoughts about healing and desire to heal come to me over and over.

I want to heal with just a touch. It is possible. Jesus did it and told his disciples (paraphrased) even greater things than this you will do. The desire keeps coming back. It is going to happen. It is possible.

I will continue to raise my vibrations, study and follow Creator's lead until I can heal with a touch because the essence of me is the essence of Source. The more I invite Oneness, the more my dreams become reality.

I always wondered if relatives or friends might judge or reject me for my healing work or for my unique spiritual expression, but it has not happened yet. My sister, Brenda, has been truly amazing, open and accepting of my talking about our family dysfunction and the traumas I have faced. I check with her before I put our family history into my books and put it out there to the public and she says, "Sure do it." What's more my truly loving sister accepts my intuitive and healing work too.

Even people I taught with in the public schools have been intrigued, not judgmental. Or if they are I have not noticed. Sometimes I laugh and say my books are full of "woo woo" stuff and my friends and family laugh with me. So far, so good.

Truthfully what I am addressing here is fear of the development of my gifts. Although I want all the gifts I can have, sometimes I feel uncertain about being different. That's too funny, because I have always been different. I believe I accept that more about me today than ever before. There is part of me that believes I can live without limits. So of course I believe I will heal with a touch one day.

Healing with a touch is healing others with God's love. This miraculous level of healing is almost beyond my imagination. At the same time, I already do it some of it. For instance, on the simplest level, a smile lifts a stranger's spirits, people feel better after a genuine hug. Then there is healing touch with intention, reassurance, and connection. Recently a client told me that merely holding my hand against her back made her back feel better before I even prayed for the healing. Such is the power of touch.

Many illnesses and wounds heal slowly and our society has us ingest all kinds of chemicals to fix them. Some help. Others create new problems. For instance, my kitty was nineteen and had arthritis. The doctor recommended prednisone. It helped, but at the same time that medication is really hard on the kidneys. So Scout got some relief and yet another health problem too. So we have both the miracle and the limitations of medicine.

Spiritual healing can be instantaneous; yet often is incremental. When people are ready to heal, if the psychological and emotional blocks are removed and if there is motivation to heal: then it works quickly. My experience is that still appears to be true.

All the healing tools available not only open the door to physical, emotional and spiritual health, they remind us of the amazing potential of unseen energy – life force (prana, chi, etc.). Application of that energy combined with intention, and openness, renders the impossible possible. Whether Reiki, acupuncture, ThetaHealing, Access Consciousness or any other modality, the tools are available. New methods will come, too.

My goal remains to heal with just a touch. Some occurs now, when will it fully develop?

Part 5:
Consciousness

Chapter 23
Surviving and Thriving

My grandmother spoke to me in spirit recently telling me that I was always special and that I am a survivor. The fact that I am the lone person who made it through the house fire makes me special. Not only surviving the fire, but then going on to thrive, to embrace life and to love as I have. Others may have shut down. I challenged life. My anger as a teen actually helped me survive, too. I continued despite my unhappiness. My grandmother advised me I must have important purpose to be the one who survived. Although, I felt extremely hurt and burdened and wanted out of this life and yet, I stuck it out.

Over the decades, some of what made it all worth it was getting to teach thousands of children and then hundreds of young soon-to-be teachers. Always, my work with children has been deeply satisfying. Working with teachers in-training was meaningful, too, because I put my years of experience and love of children and wisdom about their needs, their humanity, and their challenges into what I taught. I found I still helped children because I could influence these soon-to-be teachers to be compassionate in addition to skilled in their work. As I have said many times before, I felt privileged to do the work I have done.

One of the first children I remember influencing besides my sister Brenda was Angie, a girl whose mom was repeatedly brutalized, beaten and given detailed death threats from a boyfriend who she subsequently killed! Angie and I had become friends. I did what I could to help, was a good influence mostly because I showed her I cared. Eventually I moved out of state and we lost touch. I have wondered about her. Was she able to break the family pattern of dysfunction?

Then there were all the children I had in counseling groups while I taught school. And the work I did before that at the Teenage Crisis Line in Reno, Nevada. Plus how I protected my own sister. And later the work I did with young people at a drug and alcohol treatment center. I was able to show I cared and they knew it. They knew I believed in them.

When I worked in alcohol and drug treatment, and held counseling groups at the treatment center, I observed clients in denial, lying, in relapse, without trust, building self-trust, and just doing as told. Many of the clients had started down the path of sobriety and were clean from substances (except tobacco) even so, they showed others how to put one foot in front of the other, and how to stay out of trouble. The newer clients looked to the strong, clean and sober ones in their circles as resources for a better life.

What I noticed meant the most to the clients was realizing how much their counselors cared about them. That was more important to the clients than the tools we offered, the role plays we initiated, or even the graduation ceremonies. They were OK with the things we did in group however, most powerful was knowing we cared!

Even before retiring from teaching in the public schools, I taught meditation, healing and workshops of my own creation. What a good life. I get to empower people, show them new skills, and to help them change their limiting beliefs to see more possibility in themselves.

I have been given the opportunity to help all kinds of children, from those diagnosed with learning disabilities, emotional disabilities or intellectual disabilities. More recently

I have helped young people through alternative methodologies and worked with one extremely psychic preteen. We talk about her gifts and I help her normalize it. I help her accept herself while she experiences so many rejections in school. I show her how to reframe thinking of herself and labeling herself to focusing on the light within, her giftedness, and uniqueness as valuable and precious.

I recently began work with several children who have been mercilessly beaten, repeatedly hit, and terrorized. So it sounds like my helping others and in particular helping children began with protecting my sister. Then helping Angie and since then children who have confided in me they were being physically and/or sexually abused. I took immediate action to protect them. All were in my life for a while, not permanently, only long enough that I could give love and support in some fashion.

A final example is MJ, who, while in her early twenties, lived with my husband and me because she said she wanted to see a healthy marriage in action. She eventually moved back out on her own, yet could always count on our support. A few years later, she married and started her own family. We still see each other often and she has asked me to be "grandma" to her kids. How wonderful! I could not have children myself and yet I get to have her in my life and one grandchild so far. Really, really cool.

Chapter 24
Holy Spirit

Odd, a minute ago I was thinking the Beatles sang "When I find myself in times of trouble, Holy Spirit comes to me" but that's not right. The real lyrics were "Mother Mary comes to me."

In times of trouble, I call out "Holy Spirit, come to me, I need you" and it does. It lifts me up, raises my vibrations. With the Holy Spirit I trust my channeling is from the highest levels. With the Holy Spirit I can sing in spirit. Also it is even easier than usual to send the dark entities that show up (demons, fallen, whatever you choose to call them) to the light. The Holy Spirit makes me feel safe and light and strong, all at the same time. That unique energy, love and light is always available and remains mysterious to me.

I used to recognize the presence of the Holy Spirit because my face tingled each time It came. There were years of hearing "the tongues" in my head. Sometimes I speak in tongues along with hearing and giving the translation of their meaning. I used to feel self-conscious about having the gift of the Holy Spirit. Now it is rare, instead, I feel gratitude and joy.

Always there is a heightened mystical amazing energy that I want to hold onto and cannot. I have it for a while. I can call it to me. I do not keep it.

Will I someday be fully connected? Is it reasonable to expect that and to be of service in the world at the same time?

If fully connected in Spirit would I be so spacy I would just sit with God?

That is not the path to enlightenment I chose this time. I choose full awareness with God, i.e. God-Realization and the ability to make a difference in the world. The ability to rescue a cat, heal a child, care about a client, write a book, drive a car and go kayaking. All of that I do already. God Realization, or Self-Realization, for more precise terminology, that state of being calls me. Even as happy as I am most of the time, resting here does not feed me, but always moving into deeper understanding of and closer connection to Source does.

Chapter 25
Joy

I drove to another writing retreat today in gratitude that life is so good. It still amazes me to find myself feeling joy inside. Not every day is perfect, not anything like that, but I have joy. I never noticed joy until I was in my forties. Can you imagine that?

So thanks to my grandmother (who I mentioned earlier) for the reminder that all this time I am special and have something special to offer. Her messages show how much she loves and cares about me. What a difference it makes.

Her guidance and support makes her especially significant in my life; she was stable and present and gave unconditional love. She helped me develop into who I am, to help me leave my suffering behind and to choose to have this wonderful life.

I can say this because everything changed so much. I no longer deal with depression and the PTSD symptoms rarely kick up any more. I can laugh, teach and when things feel shitty, when I start thinking that some aspect of my life is a failure, I ponder, pout, worry, beat myself up and within less than a day, or an hour am back to my normal self, hopeful, expectant, happy, joyful and confident.

This happier self, such a long time in coming, feels right. I no longer complain about the past. It all had purpose. I am pleased I have what I have right now.

Joy shows up as living in synchronicity and living with ease. For example, I paid and registered for a 2015 writing workshop and paid for one of the three days at the hotel, but then found due to family obligations I was unable to attend. Yet it was all easily resolved because the money for the retreat and the hotel was applied to a 2016 writing retreat. This is super cool since I have already spent a boatload on classes and training in 2014-15. I thought I might have to say no to this next one and here it turns out it was already paid for. How perfect. That is living in divine timing.

So often life frustrates us because we can't make the timing or details work out the way we want. We tend to think we messed up or the world is working against us. No, that is not it. We see more clearly after time passes and it becomes apparent that the timing worked out better than we could have planned. Usually we don't have the foresight to know. For me I'd say my consciousness and my God work in tandem and I benefit.

Another example of joy is teaching and empowering others. Recently I received the opportunity to teach an Access Bars class for six youth. The class easily formed almost on its own. The students enjoyed becoming healers and helping each other.

I believe I have so much joy now because I have done lots of healing work. I do still have remnants of trauma stored in my body because I was burned in a house fire at age two and a half, molested at ages six and ten, and on top of that slapped and had my hair pulled for about ten years in childhood. When issues arise I do more clearing and healing work to move myself forward and clear the path to enlightenment.

Of course, I don't know exactly where I am on the path. I daily continue my spiritual practice so the path clears. I stay close to Creator (God) and practice remembering who I am. Probably this is everyone's journey, which they tackle fast or slow.

I must proceed and do what feels right. This is the only way to live. My spiritual practice creates connection and results in peace and joy. So yes, I have literally been through the fire and lived to not only tell about it, but to also show others through *Living Hope Steps to Leaving Suffering Behind* how they can do it too. We all can. Baby steps or big jumps, we all can move to greater and greater levels of satisfaction in our lives.

The fact that I say with assurance, life is good, shows how my view point has changed from my early years when I did not want to even live. Goes to show anything is possible.

Chapter 26
Emerging

Truth is, I am emerging. The softness, the loving being that I am is emerging now. In the past, I hid me. I did not know who I was, probably because I focused first and foremost on survival. Then I concentrated on who I should be and on who others wanted me to be, trying to get my needs met and to be what others wanted so I could feel wanted and safe.

Born sixty years ago, then surviving a house fire, my world changed dramatically at that time and it confused me. After that I minimized myself and dedicated myself to fitting in. The time has come to allow all of myself to become present. It is safe to be all of me today.

For over thirty years, I lived in two worlds both living and developing my spiritual self while wanting to be ordinary and fit in. Since my spiritual connection is the most important thing to me, it always wins. The only time I ensure true happiness and inner peace for me is when I am actively involved in connecting with the Totality or Source. Life isn't desirable for me without awareness of that something greater than I am. Today I embrace that I am different, I don't fit in with the crowd. I choose to put out into the world my spiritual side and be my unique self and all that entails.

Now I get to be my true self in the world, no longer striving to be ordinary. I chose to embrace my spiritual life and my awakening self and to share it. My uniqueness exists in order to share and to enjoy. Just as yours does.

Emerging means shifting; progressing from living in limitation to living in possibility. Along the way I assist in raising the vibrations of the planet. I assist others on their paths. I live in awareness and joy.

Chapter 27
Emptiness

Inside myself, while meditating, I notice emptiness. It is the emptiness I read about in Buddhism.

Emptiness which has more than one meaning presents a challenge to explain. Emptiness refers to the fact that ultimately, our day-to-day experience and perception of phenomena have no inherent nature by themselves. Reality is actually 'empty' of the many qualities that we normally assign to it. This relates to the concept that all that we experience here is illusion.

In me, it started as a space in the center of me or in my awareness three years ago. There was even a brief period where I experienced total emptiness and was in awe of it. The state did not maintain itself.

Now I notice a bigger space than when it originally appeared. This space is quiet. In the quiet, the chatter ceases, replaced by stillness. My needs and wants do not exist here. There is clarity if I decided to think about something. Generally though, it is a place of no questions. It is also different from the peace I experienced in my first years of meditation. This is peaceful, quiet and empty. I get to enjoy it. As the observer and aware of the emptiness I can even think a bit and ponder something; if I do that for too long, it disappears. Or does it? Maybe I simply temporarily lose awareness of it. The emptiness appears constant.

Sometimes in meditation, I see the most amazing pastels, in that blackboard-like space. Other times I see the indigo of the third eye or deep purple of the crown chakra. The rich, beautiful colors come and go. Mostly I sense emptiness and quiet. This is a space without judgment. There is little thought, so little judgment. Awe and wonder fill me and even distract me from the quiet of the emptiness. Fortunately, since it appears constant I can always go there again relax into the peace there. It feels so good to visit the emptiness of me while recognizing the wholeness of me at the same time.

My practice also includes bringing my attention to the inner spacious stillness. Few thoughts. I listen to the sound current and let it carry me. By inside, I mean in the state of conscious awareness. I access the empty quiet part of me while writing, or even while in the car. Then the stillness becomes more apparent. Anytime I move my awareness from "doing" to "being", the quiet is right there.

This appears my next stage; to bring the states of meditation into and throughout daily life. At times, it means less time sitting in meditation and being more aware or mindfulness as I go about the day. Over and over I check-in to that space of quiet emptiness or expand out as my infinite self and am aware from there. Each moment of awareness gets me out of the "realness" of daily stuff and puts me in touch with the greater truth that we have bodies and live on a planet and yet we are energy, consciousness. The physical serves us, but is not us.

Chapter 28
We are Perfection

I feel so perfect inside, how come I am not perfect outside? Are the changes I make on the inside that slow in manifesting on the outside? Jesus was the Divine manifest. Even when he appeared angry as he tossed the tables in the temple; he was fully his perfect self. I judge anger as imperfect because it does not fit with proper behavior as I was taught. Maybe his was perfect behavior for the setting and the message it sent.

The dictionary definition for perfection and success may remain constant, but mine has not. Recently I reevaluated my definition of success and wrote about it in a blog. In it I explained that my previous idea of success meant a person had millions in the bank. That describes success according to my old way of thinking. My friend shared she thought I was successful because I graduated college and did well in my career. We had different definitions. I realized the limitations in mine. I adjusted my definition of success to better match my values of love, kindness, purpose, the ability to manifest, to live in stillness and awareness.

Ideas about perfection depend on the perceiver. I think anyone enlightened is perfect. If they do what does not look perfect, it is a problem for the viewer, not for the enlightened one. Jesus and Buddha, fully awake, act from their divinity.

Buddha taught right action. This chart of the noble eightfold path might shine more light on how Buddha instructed his students to live in order to reach enlightenment.

The Noble Eightfold Path

The Buddha taught that to attain liberation one must practice wholesome:

View	Livelihood
Intention	Effort
Speech	Mindfulness
Action	Concentration

Attending to oneself in these eight areas means living in awareness of self, of thoughts, behaviors and actions. That is living consciously.

A common limitation is thinking in absolutes. Absolutes are not so absolute since we are humans capable of personal development and managing gray areas of life astutely.

Humanity actually is waking up, preparing for ascension, self-realization or enlightenment, even if it does not always appear that way. We can start at any point and have a multitude of ways to get there. A good example of a spiritual teacher who helps others "wake up" is Gary Douglas, the original founder of Access Consciousness, who does and says things that sound extremely imperfect. Deep inside he appears "empty" with little judgement, without a need to do anything, and only a desire to help others reach self-realization. He does not create karma even though he regularly says some "foul" and surprising things. In fact, his tactless comments are designed only to trigger our judgments so we can clear all that comes up freeing us from judgmentalness.

While expanding my view of enlightenment and thoughts about how that might look I notice shows like Super Soul Sunday on television where Oprah interviews people and tears up repeatedly. She feels things and lets it show with no apparent qualms.

Dain Heer, co-founder of Access Consciousness cries publicly when he is happy and also when he senses someone is unwilling to grow. These public figures allow their emotions to show while on television and the internet. I find that surprising. Not making judgments about their feelings; they are showing what they feel, just allowing it to be as it is!

As I shared earlier perfection, success, and growth is not black and white. My spine is not as straight as I would like. It is not "perfect". Actually, this statement shows my thinking that a spiritual me should have a straight back. That is a judgment. Truth is, living with any back or no back, I, like you, am an infinite being.

Not good or bad, people are a mixed bag of attributes. Comprehending the people in my life requires me not to think in black and white terms. My critical girlfriend is not all bad. She commands lots of spiritual wisdom. My spiritual teacher twenty years ago certainly helped me grow and at the same time was too controlling for my tastes. Everybody is in process. I am in process. Not thinking in black and white terms means when I think about people I acknowledge they are more than a single dimension, not all good, not all bad, actually multifaceted and complex.

I am a light being, finding the way to drop the encasement of being in the physical and removing the blindness produced by lives and experiences. Allowing my true self to shine through may actually be imminent, timely, and part of a bigger picture than I comprehend. Part of my intention is to remove the requirement to continue to reincarnate.

We may think of us as separate beings. In the quiet within me, in the awareness of the Totality, from the view of the infinite me, I am not separate from the people in this room (a writing retreat). We are one thing, oneness. In the greater truth there are no divisions, no hierarchies. We are one thing; more like a meadow, while also aware of self as a blade of grass. We are life force showing up as individuals. The unseen cadre surrounding me applauds again.

In Access Consciousness, we are encouraged to ask ourselves, "What is right about me that I am not getting?" This question works well to shift away from old thinking. It points to the change from criticizing self: from thinking I was wrong or not enough; the change from believing others had what I wanted while being uncertain I could have it. The point is I gradually changed from wounded to owning the perfection of where I have been and who I am.

Repeatedly using the question, "What is right about me that I am not getting?" opens the door to new positive perspective. This simple question triggers awareness, creating opportunity for living without criticism, without judgement. Krishnamurti said, observe self without judgement. That is kindness. Loving ourselves, recognizing our perfection remains an age old dilemma.

In the moments when I get caught up in life thinking it real; being lost in thought, in judgment, in illusion - these are just moments. When I judge myself they are just moments. They pass. I offer myself love and acceptance, moving into a state of allowance. I cancel and delete the judgment and limiting beliefs. I ask Creator for downloads to brighten my thinking, to change my outlook for the positive or to expand my insights and perspective. With a little effort, I am aware again of my infinite self, feeling whole and complete.

Remember when I said there are no mistakes. Recognizing everyone as infinite beings, directs us to the same concept, that we do not make mistakes. What we do in the big scheme of things is right for that moment, never wrong.

My conclusion: Everything *is* right about me. Everything is right about everyone, about you, too.

Chapter 29
Dream to Reality

I already talked about the dream when I sang in (what I think of as) God's voice. Now to clarify I talked about singing in the voice of God as if it will happen in the future. Actually I already do when I sing in Spirit (mostly when alone).

There was a woman in a class I taught fifteen years ago who cried and said my singing touched her deeply with the beauty of Spirit. I know it sounded beautiful to me. Inside I felt connected with something spiritual, exquisite and peaceful. Sometimes the singing is in tongues, other times it's in English.

Could it be recorded? I hope to insert a recording of it on my book's webpage. Although I still feel shy about singing in front of other people, I started voice lessons this spring to see if I can gain the confidence to progress until I can sing more comfortably in front of others.

One example of how it works: I recently had an experience working with a young woman and her mother. Every now and then I don't get full understanding of what is happening in a session until afterwards. I was inspired to sing in tongues. It felt stilted. I raised my vibrations higher and called to the Holy Spirit and still it was difficult. I let it go and moved on in our work.

Afterward I realized the problem arose first because I was unconsciously aware of dark entities that were in the room with the girl and mother and second because their purpose was to thwart her progress. After she left, I sent the entities to the light. If I had cleared them before the singing it would have been easier. Whether singing in Spirit or speaking tongues, the point was the Holy Spirit comes to assist; in this case, to release the girl from the hold of the energies that thwarted her and to allow her to feel her light.

I think I will call it singing in the voice of God; earlier I had said God's words. No, that is not it either. Sometimes it is singing love to God; other times it is just singing joyfully while aware of God. The essence, the energy that comes forth, has the power and the words. I do want to sing in Spirit in front of crowds of people. I do not need to float at the ceiling as in the dream although levitation sounds like fun, too. I totally want to bring that high spiritual vibration into the room. Not only does Spirit raise everyone's vibrations, it transforms those who are ready. I am not responsible for the outcome, only responsible for my part; alacrity, openness, high vibrations, and sharing myself. That is enough.

In asking for clarification about how it works I learned that especially high vibrations affect others in a beautiful way; they touch hearts and even brought the woman to tears in my Meeting Your Higher Self class so long ago.

Baba Ram Dass says in *Be Here Now* to use song to open the heart. In particular songs such as, *Holy, Holy, Holy; Mine Eyes Have Seen the Glory of the Coming of the Lord; and Amazing Grace*, all lift us and raise our vibrations. Singing holy songs once was a norm in India because music has always been a method of communion with Spirit. For instance singing, of Krishna and Rama (incarnations of God), a pastime that kept them close to Spirit. Ram Dass also explained what is revered is not the beauty of the voice, but the purity of the spirit of the singer.

Kirtan, the repetition in song of the holy names of God creates the process of coming into spirit. Two to five hours of

Kirtan is not unusual for the true seeker. The rhythm, repetitions, and melody creates level after level of opening. The key to this high vibrational singing is the spirit and love you bring to it.

This feels like something I am called to do. I believe it creates the kind of effect I aspire to bring the world.

Another way to hear God inside of us is through awareness of the sound current. Since learning about the sound current in the 1980s, I often follow it in meditation. Baba Ram Dass describes it as Nada Yoga, (union through sound) a technique of climbing the ladder of sound. The sounds function as tiny receivers for various planes of vibration. Each is associated with specific visual and kinesthetic experience. Every part of us is balanced and purified by focusing on these sounds.

The most frequent sound I hear resembles the sound of tiny silver cymbals tinkling. Originally when I noticed it decades ago, it was like a refrigerator's hum and then later changed to the sound of bees buzzing. Other sounds in the sound current are described as the ocean in a conch shell, melodious flute like a symphony, trumpets like thunder, rushing of wind and the highest celestial music together in harmony.

Chapter 30
Seeing

Looking deeply into people's eyes, perceiving the essence within them amazes me. Many people reveal openness, or clarity, or power or Christ consciousness. Others are shut down, or keep themselves veiled when you look in to see who the person really is.

Once as a Shaolin monk walked in front of me, for a moment I saw power in his eyes and realized at least part of him was "awake". He does not appear different most of the time; just an ordinary man on the outside. Another time at a labyrinth walking event, I glanced at a woman whose intense power in her eyes made me uncomfortable. I suspect she is a witch who cultivates power. Another variation occurred in the late 70s where a female college student's eyes shone with a light that I could only conceive was present because of her deep love of Jesus. She was the first Christian I met whose face shined with an inner glow of love and peace.

As I walked past a mirror in the middle of the night once, I stopped in my tracks stunned by the power in my eyes. Me, shining power through my eyes? I am not familiar with that. I saw a powerful being.

Generally in my past I disowned my power. Is it those past lives that made me afraid to be all that I am because of the times I was tortured or killed or captured or ostracized? Did I lose it or give it away? I suspect my early years (in this life) of trauma, tragedy and loss that created a victim's view that muted it. Maybe it was the sense of unworthiness and fear of being all you are. It is not dangerous any more to be a visionary or a healer.

I feel a sense of responsibility to keep ego from influencing my thoughts and to keep my vibrations as high as possible. I strive to be clear on what my stuff is and what is my clients' and to be open to more possibilities – not allowing limited human thinking to rule me.

Another version of seeing light is when I see nature in a whole different way. I first started noticing it while driving to work. Some mornings the light on the mountains and the cactus held a luminous vibrancy that was not always visible (not to my perception). When I see nature that way there appears to be more light present, more vibrancy in the life forms (plants) and a visible energy and clarity to it all. This also happens as I drove north of town into the hills. This kind of "seeing" maybe a noting of areas with higher vibrations. It creates a sense of awe in me.

Recently while kayaking on a lake the surface water turned luminous and sparkling. As I enjoyed the experience, the white rounded rocks below the surface began to glow too with a luminescence creating patterns that drew me to stop and observe for a while. I do not know what you call this state of seeing the energy in earth, plants and rocks. I hope I find out. I do not control it. It just occurs.

Chapter 31
Life as a Playground

On the drive to another writing retreat, I reflected on the New Age axiom "Life on Earth is a school" which promotes the thinking that we come here to learn, to experience and grow. I certainly have grown over the decades. Most people do. In contrast, if a person decides to be rigid and resistant they get that option too.

Nonetheless, now I sense life is a playground. That is a huge shift as you know if you have read my previous books (2002, 2015). This is such an amazing, beautiful planet to live on, children delight us with their innocence and beauty, and we have the love of grandparents, husbands and pets. And yes, I find life more a playground than a school house now! Maybe I am done with the schooling part of my many lives and experiences here. Maybe I get the playground experience now, a place to play with less drama, to have fun and live in peace most the time.

Fun and play, friends, animals and nature delighted all of us as children. My happy childhood memories are typically built around northern California ocean tidal pools, around fantasy experiences in the woods, and around outdoor adventures even when in the back yard. As an adult, the ocean, the woods, the sky, Havasupai in the Grand Canyon, kayaking on a lake, exploring new locations, all create that same wonder and happiness. In some ways, we haven't changed at all since childhood. Life is more a playground than a school and I love being here in it.

Life is not just work. Life is more of a playground delightfully full of sunshine, vacations, traveling, being in nature, grandbaby time, good books, good movies and all sorts of people.

We are creative beings; we build, design, and create (for me that means writing books, painting, drawing and creating classes). We are creators. You have seen it. You make things. Have you created a baby? A cake? A book? Built a house? How about a love affair that remains in your mind as an amazing and precious time period that you still savor? That is you creating. God makes it all possible by providing the natural resources, our bodies, the laws of the universe etc.

In truth, it is through our oneness that we create; we set intention, gather ingredients for biscuits and the laws of science makes them rise. I sit down at the computer to write this book and the energy of it comes from a source greater than me, also from within and from my life's experiences.

The creative force likes to create. It is fun. It is joy. So planets, universes, schools, planes, and dimensions are all created. Flower petals, puppies, mosquitos, ferns and more are all created. Life enjoying life.

Chapter 32
Unfolding Wings

For years, I wished I could be an angel. Really, I thought that would be a wonderful thing. They vibrate highly and when near, touch a special place within me with their beauty and energy. On occasion, when I get still, I notice a sensation on my back. If I knew what angels wings unfolding felt like, I'd say that is it. That is the feeling; my angel's wings are unfolding. Although, I have experienced many different entities visiting me, the angels bring some of the highest vibrations. Usually I see their wings and with that comes joy and thus distinguishes them from the others that come into my awareness. Angels vibrate at a higher rate than humans, thus they are hard to see.

A spiritual teacher, Tiffany Powers, has told me I am an angel incarnate. Receiving validation from a person I trust meant a lot after wondering about the possibility for years.

Now are humans supposed to be humans and nothing else? That sounds like limited understanding. Humans are energy. We can take form or no form as serves us at each point over the eons.

Raising our vibration is something we can do every day, and throughout the day. High vibrations in humans affect our level of awareness; affect meditations and definitely channeling. A few people vibrate at such a high rate they influence the world and the people around them by their presence. Buddha did. Jesus did. The Dalai Lama does.

There are people alive today who influence us positively through their very high vibrations. After hearing Deepak Chopra speak a few years ago, my friends and I sat and discussed the information Chopra had explained. At first, we all had such clarity and thought Chopra extraordinarily gifted at explaining complex information so we could understand it. As we talked, our understanding lessened. Eventually we gave up. I suspect Chopra's vibrations were such that he lifted us all closer to his level; thus we could understand his lecture on life. Afterwards our own vibrations returned to our normal state.

Lists can be found on the internet telling you how to raise your vibrations. When I was nineteen, I became a vegetarian; mostly the decision was instinctual; subsequently I decided to remain so in order to keep my vibrations as high as I can. I was advised it would make a difference for my meditations too.

Another way to raise vibrations easily and quickly is to sing of love to God. Christians call it singing praises. Hindus call it Kirtan – chanting/singing the names of God and devotional chants, usually in foreign languages (Sanskrit, Hindi and Gurmukhi). These spiritual practices have a profound effect on our state of mind and in particular raise our vibrations, making for blissful meditations and ecstatic states.

Maybe I am an angel, maybe not. What is most important is I live a dedicated spiritual life focused on self-realization. That in part explains why it is easy to hear and see angels, why I sense their essence in me. As I stated before, we are all infinite consciousness so although I adore the angelic beings and am delighted I have that energy too, it is only one aspect of self. Totality of self-realization calls me above all else.

Chapter 33
Revisiting Where is God?

A few years ago, two healer friends on different occasions told me some part of me still saw God as outside of me. I agreed. I feel disappointed that at any time I seek God outside of me, as they pointed out. A yoga teacher had also pointed it out when I was in my early twenties. If I had already known God inside me I would not seek. How does one switch from seeking God as something outside of self? For me it has been gradual.

I received a message recently while driving through the southern California desert to Los Angeles. I was driving along while practicing being aware of my infinite self when I asked Spirit about a pinkish, iridescent cloud that stood in the sky in front of me. It had been there a while and I wanted to know why. It appeared unique compared to the other clouds and persistent in size, position and color. I heard in response to my question the pink cloud was there to remind me to ask questions.

Although in awe of getting such a clear answer while driving on the freeway, I went ahead and asked another question: what would make the biggest difference for improving my health now? I expected an answer related to my swollen feet and ankles indicating my energy does not flow well and related to my willfulness or stubbornness.

Quite different from my more critical expectation, the astonishing answer I heard declared, "Change your ideology." I asked, "What do you mean?" As the distinctive, little, shiny cloud slowly dissolved, I heard, "Think of God as inside, not as outside."

When I was a child I was taught God is in heaven. Gradually, my sense of God is changing to God inside, in each cell, in each and every being, everywhere, in everything. Obviously my ability to fully grasp "think of God as inside, not outside" is mixed. Some part of me still thinks of God as someone to talk to outside of myself, and as someone to pray to. Who answers my questions: guides, teachers or a force that is unfathomable?

And how is it that something outside me provides answers when in truth at the same time I am an energy that is connected to all energy? I am God/Source/energy. We all are.

These questions reflect the human search for answers to universal questions. It also indicates the relevance of the metaphysical teaching (here's the short version) that we separated our consciousness (also known as the fall) from the Totality and became individuals, eventually forgetting that we are also Source. Enlightenment, Christ consciousness are all terms for the return of our awareness of who we truly are.

God is so vast that humanity has grappled with definition and description since the beginning of Earth time. One of the reasons for Jesus' life was to humanize God because we cannot connect with the totality of God. Among the many books to add to our understanding is *The Shack* where God comes in the form of three people to help a man. Many movies like *Oh God,* where God comes as George Burns because it fits John Denver's characters idea of God assist us in better grasping the God concept. Christians are taught to ask, "What would Jesus do?" Maybe it is a matter of bringing it all down to a very human level so we can connect, we can relate and we can move closer to unity with that amazing, powerful, and loving great Source.

Early in life I opened myself to a personal relationship with Jesus. His example and even more his presence, guide me. On the other hand, it inhibits my understanding if I think of God as a Being. God's essence is in all beings but it is not an "it" and not a "he". So I prefer to circumvent that dilemma and call God Source, Creator and Consciousness. These are much less limiting.

In a recent meditation I considered if I am infinite and it feels like I am. I have no edges. I do not end at any point. I also noticed that there is no other separate consciousness. It is not unpleasant; although it is not what I thought it would be like. I am aware of the consciousness that I am, but there is no God and no one else. This experience resembles the Buddhist teaching that there is no God. At the same time, I am the energy that we think of as God. I am wholeness, incredibly expansive and include that creative force.

Maybe creating is done with us, so it is not a separate thing, or not like God creates and I watch. Maybe God in me creates so I build a school. Someone else builds a bridge. What about the planets and the plants and the animals. No humans created them. God force did.

God, the Creator and life forms also as creators. Not even that separate. We are one thing and we manifest. Plants and animals do it from giving birth to building nests or dams. I can only conclude God is in everything and to fully grasp the extent again takes me to the place of considering I know me as everything. Goodness, oneness again.

Here is the visual image I get of how it started with energies from God becoming conscious singular beings like archangels, for example. Archangels make up the largest limbs and boughs extending from big tree trunk of God. Then from there the energy separated into smaller and smaller branches. We are those branches and twigs. Well maybe that is not so different than how it really is. I have heard others use the tree analogy. It helps us wrap our minds around our connection to God and each other and explains why we recognize some people when we first meet; feel close to some people and think we have known them before. Our soul family makes up the branches and twigs closest to us.

Originally, I also thought that through enlightenment I would reach a point where I could totally return to the Godhead and lose my individuality. That sounded enticing. I could just be a part of God and no longer me. Hmmm, that sounds like I did not want to be me. So I do not think that is how it works.

Eventually through study and practice I see myself as a light being with a body and realize I am an infinite being. The bodies we wear are something useful we created so we can walk on Earth, have experiences and be part of this time period.

When I guide people through the process of expanding their awareness of who they are until they recognize they are infinite, each time is an exceptional moment. Some experience awe, others simply have an experience. Possibly they hold on to too many judgments of themselves so they cannot know themselves as infinite. Some open up to a big shift and to others it appears like a first step.

What I have described throughout this book are my own realizations. For now, awareness of self as infinite is my truth while knowing my understanding will expand and grow. This has always happened and always will.

I think we are amazing, because in general we are told from the beginning of our lives that we are not connected to something greater than ourselves. In most families, we are then taught to seek that "something" outside ourselves. In religious families, we attend church or temple, follow the teachings and may or may not find God. We take in the messages from family, religion, our culture and society and then either follow them without questioning or the opposite, question everything.

I suspect the people who read my books are the ones who question everything. We also sense the dysfunction in our families and the institutions around us (schools, corporations and governments) and the inadequacy of looking outside ourselves for what will meet our needs. Then what do we do? I went searching and of course looked outside myself for the answers. I was not connected to my higher self or God self at that time so I had to look to people, to books, to religions to find my way. In that process, I gradually came to know myself better, trust myself more, realized I am not alone and discovered everything I sought and desired was already within me.

The teachings of great masters such as Buddha, Jesus, Babaji, Yogananda, Baba Ram Dass, Swami Rama, Ramana Maharaj and Sri Nisargadetta lead me to more self-love and inner peace. They guided my meditations and realizations. I could not have done it alone. Besides, there is no such thing as alone.

In revisiting where God is, I see progress as less thinking of God as outside me and more realizing that we are one thing. I may not be able to be all that God is. I can realize all of me is God.

Chapter 34
Meditation and Mindfulness

Recently after skipping my meditation for three days, I felt a little panic. Realizing my daily meditation might be slipping away scared me because of the potential loss of my connection with Spirit. A desire for closeness to God has driven me since I was a teenager. Without repeated, daily connection to a power greater than myself, I end up highly dissatisfied. In this case, in no time at all, I saw there is nothing to be afraid of. I am a spiritual being and that connection is always there, always and surprisingly easy to reconnect with.

While writing today I remembered I have formally meditated three days in a row, more my norm. Actually although I prefer regular meditation, it is not necessary to sit and meditate. Anyone can do a spiritual practice moment-to-moment rather than in formal "sitting". I happen to love sitting in the silence of meditation. I get to connect over and over to the Divine.

To sustain my meditation over the decades I used a variety of styles. I like going back to the calm and quiet of breath meditation. Other days I use the ThetaHealing technique of going to the 7th plane (reference the internet or my website www.DesertJewel.org for more information) and sinking into a heavenly energy. In that space I find everything I seek. In higher states of consciousness, I get love, inner peace, hope, answers and possibility. Often the comfort of the Holy Spirit comes in meditation and I feel the presence of God in a different powerful while loving manner.

Really what seems to be the one thing to do today beside meditation is to continuously bring my attention back to the awareness of myself as a spacious infinite being. That expansive state means moving to the Theta-brain wave state and moving into an awareness of myself here, infinite and connected to the great totality that is light and love. To clarify, this is not seated meditation, this is bringing that same kind of awareness as in meditation into daily life and activity.

Many religions teach renunciation as the preferred path; that means living without material desires, represented by disinterest and detachment from material life, and spending one's life in a peaceful, love-inspired, simple spiritual life. In *Masters of the Himalayas,* Swami Rama explained there are two paths to enlightenment. One is the renunciant, who is taken care of while seeking enlightenment. The second path, action with spirituality practiced every day in all activities, means engagement, purpose, connection, contribution, divinity and joy.

The life as a renunciant does not entice me. I am familiar with that path, having two previous lives (as seen in my meditations) when I spent all my time in bliss states while others tended my physical needs. Before remembering those lives I found myself determined to never take that path again. Determination to reach enlightenment within my ordinary life (not isolated at the mountain top) confirms my memories from those lives. Although in those two lives, I had reached God awareness, I was of no use to anyone. I helped no one but myself. Sometime since then I decided it was selfish.

This time I chose to live what Swami Rama explained as the second path, a path of action, living in the world and seeking enlightenment. That is my way. I have known it since I was about thirty years old.

The other night in face-to-face conversation in a dream, a fellow said firmly and clearly, "You need to focus on being present". The dream delivered a short, concise important message. I spend much of my day lost in thought, which creates enough distraction that I do not remember daily life's details like closing the garage door as I drive away or if I turned off the curling iron before leaving the house. Sure, a lot of people do that. Then again, I prefer to live consciously aware all the time, not intermittently.

So there is meditation and there is also daily conscious awareness - being present - which is the same as mindfulness.

I read an article that clarified for me that having awareness outside my meditation when I am in the world is what is called mindfulness. Sitting and meditating is critical but to keep that separate from my daily life is too limited, incomplete. I choose both daily mindfulness and quiet sitting in meditation.

I saved this chart from Jon Kabat-Zinn's website that I found on the internet at *http://www.getselfhelp.co.uk/mindfulness.htm*

I kept it for maybe two years knowing I liked it and wanted to do something with it. So here we are. His explanation of mindfulness provides useful clarification. Mindfulness is a hot topic and yet I had not quite grasped it. Holding the same awareness and peace I get in meditation while engaged in daily activities is living mindfully.

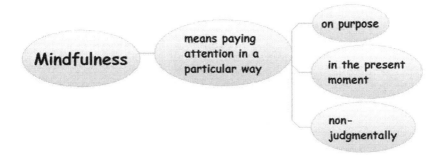

(Permission to use this chart given 7/23/2016.)

As I practice mindfulness when driving, when walking, when brushing my teeth, I realize this connects to the message I had received in a dream "Be Present." I less often am lost in thought – the opposite of mindfulness. Mindfulness means being in awareness.

For a while on my spiritual path, I judged myself as materialistic yet living a spiritual life, seeking while still following the typical American life style of consumption. Now without judgment, I live in this society of consumers while more and more detached from materialism. I have lost interest in many earthly activities and habits I thought important (well that's not entirely true, I still watch TV and movies).

I do love time in nature. I do love a deep conversation with other seekers. I love my quiet time too. Many other activities do not interest me any longer. In fact, at times it felt as if I spent too much time vacationing or going to movies and got dissatisfied. I do better if my "fun" time is well-integrated into my spiritual practice or is spent getting out into nature. My spirituality and what feeds it or what results from it are my primary drives. Certainly the equivalent of living the second path: action, living in the world, seeking enlightenment. Fortunately my work, my writing, and teaching based on my spiritual life feed my soul.

Chapter 35
Babaji

I at times found it stressful that there are so many spiritual teachers announcing what they offer on the internet. What created the stress were old beliefs that I needed something someone else has, that "I might miss out" and indicated apprehension that I must have help on my spiritual path. Of course, some spiritual paths do teach one must have a great teacher to reach enlightenment.

Two local spiritual teachers that I crossed paths with recently have high vibrations, are nice people, and have amazing gifts. I beat myself up for a while because I have not chosen to commit to either one. Truly I do have periods when I feel lost or think I need someone else to guide me and do not want to meditate.

Truth is, I am not lost. It is a matter of going through phases in my spiritual growth and not always seeing clearly when I am in the thick of one. Without clarity, I conclude I need a teacher.

I have mentioned before that knowing what state I am in and where I am going has eluded me. Jack Kornfield's book, *A Path with Heart* helped with some of it. He talks of early childhood spiritual experiences, adult life with spiritual tasks and openings, lessons, discipline, detachment, service, surrender, transitions, periods with a teacher and periods of practice on our own. He shares in depth living the cycles of spiritual growth.

I am still certain my path is meant to proceed independent of a teacher, yogi or master on this plane. This is why I do not commit to the teachers who have offered. Just like the vast amount of information on the internet: sometimes I check it out but rarely do I buy the packages offered.

When I think I would benefit from more time focused on Babaji and Jesus, I go into a meditative state and talk with them. I asked them their roles with me since I thought it unusual to have both of them.

Babaji has been my teacher, my guru, the longest. Funny I say that since time actually is not linear at all. Nonetheless, that is my view from here today. Babaji and I walked the Earth together briefly. Mostly we have met at other times and places. We have worked together side by side in other civilizations.

I do not know the number of lives we have had together because once we committed to each other he has been present with me since.

I hear and talk with him today as easily as I talk with my guides. What distinguishes his voice from the others is a knowing and a familiarity – more like recognizing his energy than his voice. Sometimes I hear him call me daughter. I do not know which life that is from. He encourages me to aspire to transcend all limitations of the physical plane. He is always present when I ask him to come.

About twenty years ago he came and told me he could help me release the sense of loneliness that had always plagued me. He said we had worked on it before and I was ready to release it. That certainly has been a relief.

Lastly I am not sure I can express how grateful I am for his presence, his love, and continuous influence. I feel extremely fortunate to have such a great teacher and will create more space/time in my life for that connection.

Babaji's role with me adds a Hindu emphasis to my spiritual development. No wonder I love Hinduism and would love to spend some time in India studying/meditating. Babaji's role with me is distinct and ancient.

Chapter 36
Jesus

I remember meeting Jesus in a cave when I was a child (in another life). I sat on the floor in the midst of a group of children when he and a few other people stepped into the cave. My heart leapt. He crouched down and talked with us about "our Father's" love. Every word went deep into my heart. I craved his teaching. I remember his face. The thought of it, the thought of him actually looking into my face has always touched me deeply inside and brought me to tears. There is a tender yet powerful overwhelming sweetness to his presence. To be that deeply loved without any degree of earning it; all that love purely because it is who he is.

The very cool thing about the presence of Jesus was not the love that he has for me but instead <u>the love that he is</u> that includes me. That kind of love is unique and reaches me at the innermost level. Baba Ram Dass explains love as a "state of being." That's what I saw in Jesus – the state of being love.

My relationship with him developed in my mid-twenties and mostly consists of talking to him and calling on him when scared. I learned to call out to him when I had nightmares. I always woke myself out of the dream by saying his name over and over until I could say it aloud and wake myself. I have never doubted his presence. Once I woke up, I would ask him to stay with me until the fear passed and I fell into a peaceful sleep.

Influenced by the "born again" Christian movement, I came to the conclusion decades ago Jesus is my friend. It makes him much more human and available to me. I even called on him daily when I was in a phase wanting to stop my anger and frustration with other drivers. I would invite him to sit in my passenger seat, which greatly influenced my inclination to swear and say all the foul things I would say about other drivers. Now about the worst thing I say while driving is that someone is an idiot and should not have a driver's license. Much improved; thank-you very much.

Thinking about this love that Jesus is and why it overwhelms me; I have asked and know others experience him that way too.

One of the reasons I feel so strongly about Jesus, results from a long time ago in a life that ended in my teens with torture and pain. As a result of that gruesome maiming, I turned away from God, light and love for I do not know how long. It was a pain filled, empty dark time. The depth of despair I experienced in that life caused me to attempt to lose myself in the dark. Although I do not remember the details of how I came out of it, I know it is again part of the depth and breadth of experience we choose.

As a result of that dark period, when I sense unconditional love especially from God, Jesus, or Kwan Yin especially feeling it through music, it creates a sense of wonder at how enormous and unending love is, then I get overwhelmed and my emotions rise up, often resulting in tears. Rather than tears of sadness, it is more like gratitude and appreciation that I still get unconditional love even though I went dark for a few lives.

I gratefully enjoy both Babaji and Jesus's roles in my many lives. Jesus's role with me is different from Babaji's. Jesus shows me love to a degree I cannot even fully imagine or absorb. He also comes to me at night and takes to the light the lost entities that show up looking for the light.

For example, the other night in a dream a woman arrived, but apparently I did not pay enough attention to her. She came by again, this time in a car; she waved and said, "It is Becca and I am still here". I realized as I woke that she was asking my acknowledgement so she could move on, and go home, after death. She was not a demon, just a lost person more like Patrick Swayze in his role in the movie *Ghost*; the character that did not go immediately into the light. Becca was asking me to show her the way. Immediately after that a guy showed up with the same issue. He said he wanted to go home, too. I called Jesus for assistance that he would be that light, that doorway for them.

Babaji and Jesus, their purposes with me each are different and divine. Both teachers have been generous, kind and consistent.

Chapter 37
Broadening Awareness

Deepak Chopra's book on tape, *God*, which I listened to on my last two drives back and forth to Los Angeles, included fascinating thought-provoking information. At the conclusion, I was astounded, because Chopra made the statement that quantum physics affected our understanding of the Law of Cause and Effect.

I checked other sources to see what he meant. Quantum physicists call it the observer effect. Scientists suggest that observation, thought and expectations influence what occurs, as demonstrated in the double-blind observation tests. It is similar to the spiritual connection between quantum physics and consciousness as presented in the film *What the Bleep Do We Know – Down the Rabbit Hole*, 2006. The film showed balls of light moving through slots differently depending on whether or not they were observed. Another test in the film showed waves or pieces of energy depending on what the observer expected to see.

I do not usually use science to understand my spiritual world, but it appears applicable here. Our bodies are a whole bunch of energy in cells held together a particular way. Then I consider why they look this particular way. Of course, because of our parents. How much is due to the soul's plan for this life? Or is created by karma? Also it looks as it does because we kept our bodies this way through thought and belief. If we change our intention and expectations, will it change what we see? Will it change what you see? It feels promising and unlimited.

Now I know God is not about looking out there; it is about my own consciousness. God is consciousness. I like that better than the time period when I used the phrase "the Force" as in "Luke, use the Force". It was the best analogy I had that people understood at the time.

God is the force, the energy that is aware and responsive. Consciousness is that too. Consciousness is energy, aware and responsive. I like it. I am consciousness, energy, aware and responsive. So are you, as is everyone. And even the space between us is consciousness, energy, awareness, and responsive. It feels like hope and love mixed together.

The energy in my cells is the same as yours and they communicate (again, quantum physics). I cannot describe what it feels like when I am in awareness of the energy inside the cells except that it is amazing and exuberant with life. I look forward to getting over the degree of awe that makes it hard to stay in the state of awareness. I will keep practicing it until it is like coming home.

This information and my experiences are all combining to know myself as God. For now in this process, I experience myself as infinite. My energy goes forever in every direction. It is an amazing, pleasant experience but it doesn't feel like God.

When I go to what Vianna Stibal (creator of ThetaHealing) calls the seventh plane, I feel a higher energy. It feels like all things are possible and like I am l loved. It feels conscious and expansive. There is not anyone there in that space, yet I am not alone. There is perfect luminous energetic light there.

When I think about my understanding of God, I suspect it fluctuates sometimes more intellectual, other times more "knowing", I know that I am God, not separate from and seeking. I know it because God is everywhere and in me. I could not exist without that life force. Is it prana? Chi? Is it in my mitochondria? If it is me, how come I cannot speak easily and definitively about it? Lots of people have said in the past that God is elusive. I do not want to go with that. God is energy. I am energy. We are the same thing.

I wonder if it has to do with connection. When I feel myself as infinite extending out across universes, I know I am God but I don't feel like what I think God feels like. Maybe I expect God to be a separate consciousness. That must be part of the problem, part of thinking as taught in church. The most significant value I can find in that kind of learning is then knowing the direction to travel to find what I did not have and desperately sought.

I created this book, this home, this life, this body. Therefore, I am a creator too. Right now it looks like a small scale creator. Nonetheless, all of us are creators.

We are simply creative beings, creating and reinforcing our lives with our thoughts. Also we plan, design, build, and create everything from buildings, to homes, to cities, to an ascetically pleasing meal, to new books, and new classes. There is no limit. Our creativity expressed on so many levels builds our personal lives and our world.

Can I figure out life through reasoning? Do I solely do it through decades of meditation? Do I seek spiritual highs and revelations? Or do I do it like those in Access Consciousness where they remove all obstacles, all points of view that define them and become fully awake?

What I have gained through a spiritual practice with Buddhism, ThetaHealing, Access Bars and Access Consciousness has added to the sense of emptiness. When I sit in meditation the stillness is larger than before. I just enjoy the quiet in awareness and am in awe of it. There is less to my personality than there once was. Maybe that is not how to explain it. I feel empty in a good way. I have preferences, and yes, fears still come up. While at the same time, there is an ease where little matters. In traditional thinking, that is not a good thing, but I say it is. It is being in an easy space where you do the next thing guided by your awareness. It is a matter of asking what I am to do next.

Life is easier; that is the point. There is less internal pressure to do a specific thing. I like it. If I want to reach a goal I set a goal then do what is necessary in a timely fashion to achieve it.

Part of this change means I have fewer pressing wants. I would love new faucets in the master bath and a new rug for the living room floor, but it does not actually matter. When it is timely I will take care of it.

This reminds me of living in the opposite space, in addiction. At one time, compulsive shopping controlled me, even if I had worked all day. I taught in the public school system and sometimes felt I had to go shopping and look for clothes on the way home from work. My feet hurt from walking on concrete all day and still I needed to shop. My credit cards all held balances and I needed to shop anyway. I did not have to have clothes at that moment, I needed to shop. That's a shopping addiction.

Thank God that compulsion subsided. It doesn't drive me like it once did. I do buy things as needed, only when convenient, with intention and when I choose to add to my home or wardrobe - not by compulsion to numb out and not by the obsession to obtain.

When I talk with Creator about my heart's desire, my preferences always shrink because what I truly want is what my God wants. When attuned to God, I feel inspired and happy. I prefer that my guidance and direction come from that connection. Then I am content.

Life comes so easily, fears and compulsions fall away signaling the results of living the Buddhist Eightfold Path and living as Jesus would (all to the best of my ability) gradually moving into self-realization, the reward of years of dedication and practice.

Chapter 38
New Possibilities

I still aspire to expand my knowing so that it does not have God outside me and me asking for growth/ideas/help etc. I prefer to see and know all the time how we are the same thing. I am only an expression of it in this form (as Lynne). All I have to do is pause, look inside and the answers arise. Or to be in allowance that what I have requested will appear in divine timing.

Maybe once there is full realization "knowing" and connection stops being progressive. Although recently, I was told Buddha declared himself enlightened six times as if he thought each a deeper enlightenment than those previous. Nonetheless, I am enjoying the moments of realization, mine and my students and clients for now. The transformations I describe show progress in a spiritual journey.

This progression I am referring to is like a slow dawning that things are not in actuality the way we perceive them. It has been pointed out by scientists that objects are not solid, and that water responds molecularly to human statements. Albert Einstein explained it especially well, "Reality is merely an illusion, although a very persistent one".

We know that children sometimes tell their parents about their past life memories and are dismissed. Our lack of truth is not much different from when humans were taught the world was flat. Yet yogis demonstrate levitation, Maharishi University students walk through walls; people bend spoons with their minds. How many more misconceptions limiting our life experience hamper us? What might happen if we challenge what holds us back from embracing all of our potential?

Mostly we adhere to what we have been taught by our families and by our schools. Not wrong or bad, they taught what they knew. If they had known different they might have taught us differently, may have given us a broader range of truths. Ask yourself everyday, "What else is possible"? Expect and allow greater possibilities to arrive while letting go of what they should look like.

A constructive medium, film especially helps us expand our thinking. It introduces possibilities as if they already exist. Science-fiction excels in presenting new concepts and possibilities. On occasion, we remember seeing something in a science-fiction piece and later seeing it come into reality. This even occurred through cartoons. Many of the futuristic features such as talking to computers that once amused us in the cartoon "The Jetson's" is now common place.

Or consider the film, the quite complex *Cloud Atlas* which showed us the progression of a group of souls, killers and heroes, kindness and cruelty through centuries. The film shows the complexity of several souls' progression, maybe not as linear as some might have thought. Another example that got my attention because of the many representations of metaphysical concepts, *What Dreams May Come* with Robin Williams for instance, depicts the Akashic Records as an enormous library. Or look at how time is only relative to place in *Intersteller*. More recently, the film *Arrival* presents past, present, future as all present in each moment not linear; a film worth seeing more than once in order to absorb this concept. Film, the perfect medium to bring new ideas to life, or to concretize metaphysical concepts.

Chapter 39
Eternal Luminous Being

True self is life force - I know this on many levels. Last week I had a beautiful experience channeling for a ThetaHealer (referred to as the message in chapter seven). When she asked who was speaking, the energy told her it was life force. It did not identify itself with a name, said it had never worn a human body and could be considered part of a coalition, indicating that its name and that labeling it was less important. Instead, it encouraged her to see herself in a new light; to no longer identify with the drama of understanding her many lifetimes, aliens, missions, etc. explaining that the time to figure out all that was over. It explained it is time to change your view. Rather than seeing you as the individual working through lives and figuring out how to balance karma and understand all that transpired, let that go. You no longer have karma or when you create it, it is balanced quickly and you can even see what the cause was.

Let that in. That is true for most of us now. That may be true for you, too.

They encouraged her to see herself as a conscious being, a light being.

Permanent knowing of self as life force, as Consciousness is my ultimate goal. As I know now, "I Am That". This awareness came in stages, gradually over years. It does not have to be that way for someone else; it simply has been for me.

One of the first stages occurred years ago, when I discovered in the guided meditations by Deepak Chopra that my awareness shifted when he asked <u>who was it inside me that was aware that I was thinking</u>. At that moment, I realized I hear and observe thinking while I am actually separate from it. I am the observer. Thinking occurs on the surface. I, the observer, exist beyond that. This brought realization that I am something beyond my thoughts. I found it mind-expanding and exciting. I knew I moved a smidge closer to what the masters know.

Michael A. Singer in *The Untethered Soul* explains it beautifully. He tells us:

> As you go deeper into yourself, you will naturally come to realize that there is an aspect of your being that is always there and never changes. This is your sense of awareness, your consciousness. ... You are not your thoughts; you are aware of your thoughts. You are not your emotions; you feel your emotions. You are not your body; you look at it in the mirror and experience this world through its eyes and ears. You are the conscious being who is aware that you are aware of all these inner and outer things.

The latest stage has been a shift to know I am infinite. I had had other moments of realization when my consciousness moved out into the universe and recognized "I Am That". Instead of thinking of seeking God as something outside myself I knew in the meditation I am part of the huge, nebulous, peaceful and awe-inspiring Consciousness.

Next, Access Consciousness took me to a new place. Their expand-to-your-infinite-self exercise created my I-am-an-infinite-being realization. Another Access Consciousness guided meditation showed me the life force in my cells and atoms and the life force in the chair's atoms is the same energy.

It is the prana we absorb in breath work. It is the chi we gather and move around in tai chi and chi gong.

This also means I am the life force that causes the cells to be alive, causes the breath to move in and out, and allows awareness of self all at the same time and also sustains the body I created for this life. Part of the shift was going from knowing this interconnectedness intellectually to a constant, deeper level of knowing.

This is oneness. Describing developing awareness of oneness with all things challenges me to say the least.

Next came integrating oneness with all beings, all cells, all life and my infinite self that contains all universes.

These discoveries have been a process. I started meditating when I was about twenty. This evolution took a while. It sped up a few years ago prior to 2012 and since has sped up even more.

Chapter 40
True Self

I am a light being finding ways to drop the encasing blindness created by lives of physical experience and now allow my true self to shine through. This is what my pure original self wants. Let me be seen. Let my light shine. Release the fear. No holding back. Sensing my true self – I go there. When referring to my true self, I am referring to a luminous being, light, conscious, life force energy and awareness. I suspect that most people also look like luminous orbs of light.

My body is not who I am; it is a vehicle for what I do. Reaching people through my body as Lynne is in part why I am here. The first twenty-five years of my life burned off intense karma and created conditions to form my personality as it is. Then I did the work releasing beliefs and patterns so my true self could come through.

The next thirty-five years appeared to be about personal and spiritual growth, and overcoming childhood trauma all while enjoying my life as a special education teacher in the public schools and discovering the joy of life through counseling, healing, teaching and all the alternative healing and teaching work. My purpose is to help others have the life they want; a life that brings them joy, to empower them to be free of the old stale beliefs that hamper and as always to show love.

I am ready to release the need to be identified by my name, even my soul's name, my personality or sixty years of history.

I recently studied with a group that suggested the concept of having a higher self is another limiting illusion of this plane of existence. I admit that rocked my boat; part of me says no it is not an illusion and wants to stomp her feet. Yes, in truth I have to say higher self is an illusion too; a functional construct useful for contemplating our relationship to God, useful if you want to stay within the constraints of this world. I do not.

I am light and Source energy. I pent it up in the density of this life and so many lives. I have finished playing out the dance of experiences. I am free to realize the beautiful light that I am, a full light being realizing that light is love, pure love. The same sweetness I feel in others, in my clients and students is in me, too. The essence of us is the essence of God, love, strong, creative, powerful, and indestructible while also tender, quiet and peaceful.

I am responsible for my part in the universe, my part in creation, my part in the many lives. But I am not that. I am not any of the identities; I am pure energy!

When I expanded my awareness and went out into the universe, I knew I am infinite and include everything, the universe and all it's contents. Then I am just the "I am" and it is quiet. When I contemplate the life force inside myself, I know it is what I truly am. I consider that it is the same life force in all cells, all things, all beings, all life then excitement fills me.

We all are life force. Again I hear the cadre of spirits (guides, masters, ancestors and angels) with me clapping with delight. This is similar to who I channeled: no names, no physical lives for some, purely life force. The names and identities represent ego. We get to be free of that.

Now I prefer to let go of my old identities and live aware of self as Consciousness. It means going bigger. I am more than I thought, not a single human being. Look at all the thousands of lives we have had. I prefer not to identify as any one of them, not even as this one. I prefer to know myself as that which chose and created and experienced all these lives. I am that which is continuous throughout space and time. I am not the equivalent of a blade of grass in a field, not the equivalent of one in a mass of people. I am the life force in the meadow; love and pure Consciousness. As you are.

This view is awake, aware and so different from the old belief I carried, implanted by family, ancestors, other lives, or aliens which told me "you can't be all that." The truth is I am all that. Right now as I said I am wearing this body perfectly created for this life, this incarnation. I am so much more than a body, a mind, a personality, or a brain.

Awareness brings change, stops old patterns, and prevents new karma. Mindfulness creates awareness and the possibility of observing without judgment.

It is easy to go there in meditation, within is emptiness, and mostly silence. I am in awe of the quiet and tranquility. My body does not contain me. Nor can yours contain you.

I Am That, the awareness in the emptiness. Emptiness is that space that opens inside where I held fear and lack and junk once upon a time. All released through studying, healing, counseling, meditation, journaling, allowing, love, seeking, ThetaHealing and Access Consciousness. Some call it spaciousness. I agree, and for me it includes peace.

I am comforted to know I am not the first or the last to ask about these things. Many have gotten further in their understanding than me. Being a seeker and becoming a realizer must be enough for now. Chopra says consciousness is the next state of our evolution. Whether called consciousness, awareness, or self-realization, all are the same and contain high degrees of spiritual development. That is who we are and this is the time period for all of us to evolve into true self. We finally get to move from seeking to enlightenment.

And just for fun remember as Baba Ram Dass prompted us: Know God, see divine light, experience bliss, converse with God and know your zip code.

These are many of the tools I found especially helpful over the years. For fun try:

Meditate	Ask questions	Show your love
Guided meditations	Ask for illumination while sleeping	Help someone else
Breathe slowly, deeply	Read a book from my suggested list	Help animals
Chant	Shed your stuff	Garden
Practice Being while Doing	Shed your story	See a film from the suggested films list
Stop judging yourself	Get your Bars run (Access Bars)	Sing
Use angel cards	Surrender (let go)	Try something new
Practice nonjudgement	Study yoga	Allow yourself to just rest
Practice Self-acceptance	Patience with your self	Walk barefoot in the grass
Practice, stopping and asking, then Listen deeply	Learn to know what your intuition tells you	Learn to get your own Guidance
Look for the Light	Call out to the Holy Spirit	Meditate on the sound current
Ask questions of Source and journal the responses	Pause and listen to the inner silence	Look at your eyes in mirror and tell yourself you love you.

References and Suggested Films

Film: *Arrival, Cloud Atlas, Ghost, Intersteller, Matrix, Oh God, What Dreams May Come, What the Bleep Do We Know*

References and Suggested Reading

Chopra, Deepak	God, 2013
Gawain, Shakti	Awakening A Daily Guide to Conscious Living, 1991
Haich, Elisabeth	Initiation, 1974
Heer, Dain	Being You, Changing the World
Kornfield, Jack	A Path with Heart, 1993
MacLaine, Shirley	What If… A Lifetime of Questions, Speculations, Reasonable Guesses, and a Few Things I Know for Sure, 2013
Nisargadetta, Maharaj	I Am That Talks with Sri Nisargadatta Maharaj 1988
Nisargadetta, Maharaj	The Experience of Nothingness Sri Nisargadatta Maharaj's Talks on Realizing the Infinite 1996 (edited by Robert Powell, Ph.D.)

Ram Dass, Baba	Be Here Now, 1971
Ram Dass, Baba	Polishing the Mirror, 2014
Seifer, Nancy & Viereg, Martin	Whenthesouldawakens.org/ living as a soul
Singer, Michael A.	The Untethered Soul, 2007
Rama, Swami	Living with Masters of the Himalayas, 2007
Virtue, Doreen	Archangels and Ascended Masters, 2003
Young, William Paul	The Shack, 2008

Book Club Discussion Questions:

1. Who do you think is the audience for *Unfolding the Mystery of Self*?

2. How is this book useful?

3. Why the subtitle *We are Never Alone*?

4. The author says there are no mistakes. What is your opinion?

5. She also says "What is right about me that I'm not getting?" What do you think of that statement?

6. The author talked about life as having been difficult leaving her unhappy. How did she move from that state of mind to her more optimistic outlook?

7. Is enlightenment possible without living a monastic life?

8. The author suggests everyone is intuitive, but can they have visions and intuitive dreams?

9. What is the emptiness, stillness and inner peace that she referred to? How did she get there?

10. It has been said everyone needs a guru or a spiritual teacher? What do you think?